GRILL

THE AUSTRALIAN
Women's Weekly

GRILL
grill-pan + barbecue

acp
books

contents

Savour the goodness of grilling in more ways than just on your tastebuds: grilling is not only delicious, but also one of the easiest and healthiest ways to cook. Under the grill, you can melt or brown food to perfection. Fully preheat the grill before placing the food under; this can take 5-10 minutes. Line the tray beneath the grill rack with aluminium foil to keep cleaning to a minimum.

Using a grill pan on top of the stove is an excellent way to get char-grill results without resorting to the outdoors. Use a good quality, cast-iron grill pan for best results. Spray or brush with a little oil before heating. Heat the grill pan to very hot before adding the food, then cook for a few minutes without moving for clearly defined char-grill marks. Grilling produces a lot of smoke, so have an extractor fan turned on.

The barbecue is the embodiment of easy, relaxed entertaining and is incredibly versatile – perfect for cooking vegies, fish, poultry and meat. Use direct or indirect heat to cook small or large cuts respectively. Ensure the hotplate is very hot before you add the food, and for tender results, allow meat to rest, covered, in a warm place before serving.

under
the grill

Bacon and tomato scallops

15g butter
3 rashers rindless bacon (195g), chopped finely
2 small egg tomatoes (120g), seeded, chopped finely
2 green onions, sliced thinly
24 scallops, roe removed (600g), on the half shell
⅓ cup (25g) coarsely grated parmesan cheese

1 Melt butter in medium frying pan; cook bacon, stirring, about 5 minutes or until bacon is crisp. Remove from heat; stir in tomato and onion.
2 Preheat grill.
3 Remove scallops from shells; rinse and dry shells. Return scallops to shells; grill scallops about 5 minutes or until cooked. Top scallops with bacon mixture and cheese; grill until cheese melts.

preparation time 15 minutes **cooking time** 12 minutes **serves** 4
nutritional count per serving 9.9g total fat (5g saturated fat); 836kJ (200 cal); 2g carbohydrate; 25.5g protein; 0.5g fibre

Scallops with warm rocket pesto

40g baby rocket leaves
¼ cup (35g) roasted pistachios
1 clove garlic, quartered
1 teaspoon finely grated lemon rind
2 teaspoons lemon juice
¼ cup (60ml) olive oil
¼ cup (60ml) warm water
2 tablespoons finely grated parmesan cheese
24 scallops, roe removed (600g), on the half shell

1 Blend or process rocket, nuts, garlic, rind and juice until smooth. With motor operating, gradually add oil in thin, steady stream until pesto is almost smooth. Stir in the water and cheese.
2 Preheat grill.
3 Remove scallops from shells; rinse and dry shells. Return scallops to shells; grill scallops about 5 minutes or until cooked. Top scallops with pesto; grill until pesto bubbles.

preparation time 15 minutes **cooking time** 6 minutes
serves 4 (makes ½ cup pesto)
nutritional count per serving 20.3g total fat (3.4g saturated fat); 1158kJ (277 cal); 2.6g carbohydrate; 20.7g protein; 1.1g fibre

Salmon with macadamia mayonnaise

2 egg yolks
½ teaspoon coarse cooking salt
½ teaspoon mustard powder
2 tablespoons lemon juice
½ cup (125ml) light olive oil
⅓ cup (45g) roasted macadamias, chopped coarsely
4 x 200g salmon fillets

1 Preheat grill.
2 To make macadamia mayonnaise, combine egg yolks in medium bowl with salt, mustard and half the juice. Gradually add oil in thin, steady stream, whisking constantly until mixture thickens. Whisk in remaining juice and nuts.
3 Grill salmon, skin-side up, until skin is crisp; turn, grill until cooked as desired. Serve with macadamia mayonnaise.

preparation time 10 minutes **cooking time** 10 minutes **serves** 4
nutritional count per serving 54.1g total fat (9.2g saturated fat); 2725kJ (652 cal); 0.8g carbohydrate; 41.5g protein; 0.7g fibre

Fish fillets with fennel salad

4 x 200g white fish fillets, skin-on
2 medium red capsicums (400g), chopped coarsely
2 small fennel (400g), trimmed, sliced thinly
½ cup (60g) seeded black olives
⅓ cup coarsely chopped fresh basil
2 tablespoons olive oil
1 tablespoon balsamic vinegar

1 Preheat grill.
2 Cook fillets, under hot grill, turning once, until cooked through.
3 Meanwhile, combine remaining ingredients in medium bowl.
4 Serve fillets with salad.

preparation time 10 minutes **cooking time** 10 minutes **serves** 4
nutritional count per serving 13.9g total fat (2.7g saturated fat);
1409kJ (337 cal); 8.6g carbohydrate; 42.9g protein; 2.8g fibre
tip we used blue eye in this recipe, but you can use any firm white fish.

Asian burgers

1 teaspoon peanut oil
10cm stick fresh lemon grass (20g), chopped finely
1 small red onion (100g), chopped finely
½ teaspoon five-spice powder
½ teaspoon dried chilli flakes
1 tablespoon fish sauce
2 teaspoons finely grated lime rind
140ml can coconut cream
2 tablespoons crunchy peanut butter
500g chicken mince
1 cup (70g) stale breadcrumbs
¼ cup finely chopped fresh coriander
1 egg
1 medium carrot (120g)
1 lebanese cucumber (130g)
4 hamburger buns

1 Preheat grill.
2 Heat oil in small frying pan; cook lemon grass and onion, stirring, until onion softens. Add five-spice, chilli, sauce, rind and coconut cream; bring to the boil. Boil sauce mixture, uncovered, until reduced by half; cool 5 minutes.
3 Combine half of the sauce with peanut butter in small bowl. Combine remaining sauce with chicken, breadcrumbs, coriander and egg in large bowl; use hands to shape chicken mixture into four patties.
4 Using vegetable peeler, slice carrot and cucumber into thin strips.
5 Cook patties under hot grill, turning once, until cooked through.
6 Meanwhile, halve buns horizontally; toast, cut-sides up, under hot grill. Spread peanut butter mixture on bun tops; sandwich patties, carrot and cucumber between bun halves.

preparation time 15 minutes **cooking time** 25 minutes **serves** 4
nutritional count per serving 29.5g total fat (11.5g saturated fat); 2746kJ (657 cal); 54.9g carbohydrate; 39.7g protein; 7g fibre

Cajun chicken with pineapple salsa

1 tablespoon sweet paprika
1 teaspoon cayenne pepper
2 teaspoons garlic powder
2 teaspoons dried oregano
1 tablespoon olive oil
8 chicken thigh fillets (880g)
pineapple salsa
4 rashers rindless bacon (260g)
1 small pineapple (800g), chopped finely
1 fresh small red thai chilli, chopped finely
¼ cup coarsely chopped fresh flat-leaf parsley
1 medium red capsicum (200g), chopped coarsely
¼ cup (60ml) lime juice
1 teaspoon olive oil

1 Combine spices, oregano and oil in large bowl with chicken.
2 Preheat grill.
3 Make pineapple salsa.
4 Cook chicken, under hot grill, turning once, until cooked through.
5 Serve chicken with salsa and lemon wedges, if desired.
pineapple salsa cook bacon, under hot grill until crisp; drain then chop coarsely. Place bacon in medium bowl with remaining ingredients; toss gently to combine.

preparation time 15 minutes **cooking time** 15 minutes **serves** 4
nutritional count per serving 6.8g total fat (2.0g saturated fat);
502kJ (120 cal); 2.3g carbohydrate; 12.3g protein; 0.6g fibre

Spicy veal pizzaiola

2 teaspoons olive oil
2 cloves garlic, crushed
4 slices pancetta (60g), chopped finely
¼ cup (60ml) dry white wine
700g bottled tomato pasta sauce
1 teaspoon dried chilli flakes
4 x 170g veal cutlets
75g baby spinach leaves

1 Heat oil in large saucepan; cook garlic and pancetta, stirring, about
5 minutes. Add wine; cook, stirring, until wine is reduced by half. Add sauce
and chilli; simmer, uncovered, about 15 minutes or until sauce thickens.
2 Meanwhile, preheat grill.
3 Cook veal, under hot grill, turning once, until cooked as desired.
4 Remove sauce from heat; stir in spinach. Serve veal topped with sauce,
accompanied with pasta, if desired.

preparation time 10 minutes **cooking time** 20 minutes **serves** 4
nutritional count per serving 14.6g total fat (2.8g saturated fat);
1555kJ (372 cal); 18.8g carbohydrate; 36.3g protein; 4.3g fibre
tip the pizzaiola sauce recipe makes enough to accompany 375g of
the cooked pasta of your choice, or you can cover and reserve it in the
fridge for use within three days.

Lemon chilli pork with italian brown rice salad

2 teaspoons finely grated lemon rind
2 tablespoons lemon juice
½ teaspoon dried chilli flakes
1 tablespoon olive oil
4 x 240g pork cutlets
italian brown rice salad
1 cup (200g) brown long-grain rice
1 medium red capsicum (200g), chopped finely
½ cup (60g) seeded black olives, chopped coarsely
2 tablespoons drained capers, rinsed
½ cup coarsely chopped fresh basil
⅓ cup coarsely chopped fresh flat-leaf parsley
2 tablespoons lemon juice
1 tablespoon olive oil

1 Combine rind, juice, chilli, oil and pork in medium bowl. Cover; refrigerate until required.
2 Make italian brown rice salad.
3 Preheat grill.
4 Cook pork, under hot grill, turning once, until cooked through. Serve pork with rice salad.
italian brown rice salad cook rice in large saucepan of boiling water, uncovered, until tender; drain. Rinse under cold water; drain. Place rice in large bowl with remaining ingredients; toss gently to combine.

preparation time 35 minutes **cooking time** 50 minutes **serves** 4
nutritional count per serving 14.7g total fat (2.9g saturated fat); 1969kJ (471 cal); 46.4g carbohydrate; 35.7g protein; 3g fibre

Lamb, bocconcini and gremolata stacks

4 x 150g lamb leg steaks
1 tablespoon olive oil
1 large red capsicum (350g)
2 tablespoons lemon juice
100g bocconcini cheese, sliced thinly
gremolata
2 teaspoons finely grated lemon rind
2 cloves garlic, chopped finely
2 tablespoons finely chopped fresh basil

1 Preheat grill.
2 Make gremolata.
3 Using meat mallet, gently pound lamb between sheets of plastic wrap until 1cm thick. Heat oil in large frying pan; cook lamb, in batches, until cooked as desired. Place lamb on oven tray.
4 Meanwhile, quarter capsicum, discard seeds and membranes. Roast under grill, skin-side up, until skin blisters and blackens. Cover capsicum pieces in plastic or paper for 5 minutes; peel away skin then slice flesh thickly. Combine capsicum and juice in small bowl.
5 Divide capsicum and cheese among lamb steaks; grill about 5 minutes or until cheese melts.
6 Serve stacks sprinkled with gremolata and, if desired, a rocket salad.
gremolata combine ingredients in small bowl.

preparation time 15 minutes **cooking time** 20 minutes **serves** 4
nutritional count per serving 16.7g total fat (6.8g saturated fat); 1346kJ (322 cal); 3.4g carbohydrate; 38.8g protein; 1.2g fibre

Lamb cutlets niçoise

12 french-trimmed lamb cutlets (600g)
1 large cos lettuce, chopped coarsely
420g can white beans, rinsed, drained
3 medium tomatoes (450g), cut into wedges
lemon anchovy dressing
4 drained anchovy fillets, chopped finely
3 cloves garlic, crushed
3 teaspoons finely grated lemon rind
⅓ cup (80ml) lemon juice
⅓ cup (80ml) olive oil

1 Make lemon anchovy dressing.
2 Preheat grill.
3 Combine lamb and 2 tablespoons of the dressing in large bowl.
4 Cook lamb, under hot grill, turning once, until cooked as desired.
Remove from heat; drizzle with 1 tablespoon of the dressing, cover to
keep warm.
5 Place lettuce, beans and tomato in large bowl with remaining dressing;
toss gently to combine. Serve lamb with salad.
lemon anchovy dressing   place ingredients in screw-top jar; shake well.

preparation time 10 minutes **cooking time** 20 minutes **serves** 4
nutritional count per serving 33g total fat (8.8g saturated fat);
1852kJ (443 cal); 9.9g carbohydrate; 24.8g protein; 5.2g fibre

Paprika-dusted lamb chops with greek salad

8 lamb loin chops (800g)
2 teaspoons sweet paprika
1 medium red capsicum (200g), chopped coarsely
1 medium green capsicum (200g), chopped coarsely
2 medium tomatoes (300g), chopped coarsely
200g fetta cheese, cut into 2cm pieces
¼ cup firmly packed fresh flat-leaf parsley leaves
2 tablespoons olive oil
1 tablespoon lemon juice

1 Preheat grill.
2 Sprinkle lamb with paprika. Cook lamb, under hot grill, turning once, until cooked as desired. Cover; stand 5 minutes.
3 Meanwhile, place capsicums, tomato, cheese, parsley, oil and juice in large bowl; toss gently to combine.
4 Divide salad and lamb among serving plates; serve with lemon wedges, if desired.

preparation time 15 minutes **cooking time** 10 minutes **serves** 4
nutritional count per serving 38.6g total fat (15.9g saturated fat);
2236kJ (535 cal); 4.4g carbohydrate; 42.8g protein; 1.9g fibre

Open steak sandwich with roasted capsicum and ricotta

2 medium red capsicums (400g)
¾ cup (180g) ricotta cheese
2 tablespoons coarsely chopped fresh chervil
2 teaspoons lemon juice
4 x 125g beef minute steaks
1 tablespoon cracked black pepper
4 slices rye sourdough bread (180g)
1 tablespoon olive oil
2 cloves garlic, crushed
40g baby rocket leaves

1 Preheat grill.
2 Quarter capsicums; discard seeds and membranes. Roast under hot grill, skin-side up, until skin blisters and blackens. Cover capsicum pieces in plastic or paper 5 minutes; peel away skin.
3 Meanwhile, combine cheese, chervil and juice in small bowl.
4 Sprinkle beef with pepper; cook under hot grill, turning once, until cooked as desired.
5 Brush one side of each bread slice with combined oil and garlic; toast both sides under hot grill. Spread bread with cheese mixture; top with capsicum, beef then rocket.

preparation time 15 minutes **cooking time** 15 minutes **serves** 4
nutritional count per serving 19.3g total fat (7.6g saturated fat);
1793kJ (429 cal); 25g carbohydrate; 36.8g protein; 3.9g fibre

Za'atar-spiced veal chops with fattoush

4 x 200g veal loin chops
za'atar
1 tablespoon sumac
1 tablespoon roasted sesame seeds
2 teaspoons finely chopped fresh thyme
1 tablespoon olive oil
1 teaspoon dried marjoram
fattoush
2 large pitta breads (160g)
4 medium tomatoes (600g), cut into wedges
2 lebanese cucumbers (260g), seeded, sliced thinly
1 medium green capsicum (200g), cut into 2cm pieces
3 green onions, sliced thinly
1 cup coarsely chopped fresh flat-leaf parsley
½ cup coarsely chopped fresh mint
½ cup (125ml) olive oil
¼ cup (60ml) lemon juice
2 cloves garlic, crushed

1 Preheat grill.
2 Make za'atar and fattoush.
3 Cook veal under hot grill, turning once, until cooked as desired.
Sprinkle about a tablespoon of the za'atar equally over the veal; serve
with fattoush.
za'atar combine ingredients in small bowl.
fattoush grill bread until crisp; break into small pieces. Combine tomato,
cucumber, capsicum, onion and herbs in large bowl. Just before serving,
toss bread and combined oil, juice and garlic into salad.

preparation time 15 minutes **cooking time** 20 minutes **serves** 4
nutritional count per serving 38.9g total fat (5.9g saturated fat);
2587kJ (619 cal); 27.8g carbohydrate; 36.5g protein; 17.1g fibre
tips sumac is a purple-red, astringent spice ground from berries growing
on shrubs that flourish wild around the Mediterranean; adds a tart,
lemony flavour. Can be found in Middle Eastern food stores.
While za'atar is easy to make, it can also be purchased in Middle Eastern
food shops and some delicatessens.

Scotch fillet with pepper thyme sauce

4 x 200g beef scotch fillet steaks
2 teaspoons olive oil
1 medium brown onion (150g), chopped finely
1 trimmed celery stalk (100g), chopped finely
½ cup (125ml) dry white wine
300ml cream
1 tablespoon mixed peppercorns, crushed
1 tablespoon coarsely chopped fresh thyme

1 Preheat grill.
2 Cook beef, under hot grill, turning once, until cooked as desired.
Cover to keep warm.
3 Meanwhile, heat oil in medium frying pan; cook onion and celery,
stirring, until vegetables soften. Add wine; stir until liquid is reduced by
half. Add cream and peppercorns; bring to the boil. Reduce heat; simmer,
uncovered, stirring occasionally, about 5 minutes or until sauce thickens
slightly. Remove from heat; stir in thyme.
4 Serve beef with sauce, and accompanied with chunky chips, if desired.

preparation time 10 minutes **cooking time** 15 minutes **serves** 4
nutritional count per serving 46.7g total fat (26.3g saturated fat);
2658kJ (636 cal); 5g carbohydrate; 44.2g protein; 1.4g fibre

Grilled pork medallions with capsicum cream sauce

1 medium red capsicum (200g)
1 medium tomato (150g), halved, seeded
2 teaspoons olive oil
1 small brown onion (80g), chopped finely
1 clove garlic, crushed
½ trimmed celery stalk (50g), chopped finely
2 tablespoons water
1 teaspoon finely chopped fresh rosemary
4 x 150g pork medallions
½ cup (125ml) cream

1 Preheat grill.
2 Quarter capsicum; discard seeds and membranes. Roast capsicum and tomato under grill, skin-side up, until capsicum skin blisters and blackens. Cover capsicum and tomato pieces with plastic or paper for 5 minutes; peel away skins then slice capsicum thickly.
3 Meanwhile, heat oil in large frying pan; cook onion, garlic and celery until softened. Add capsicum, tomato and the water; cook, uncovered, 5 minutes. Remove from heat; stir in rosemary.
4 Cook pork, under hot grill, turning once, until cooked through. Cover to keep warm.
5 Blend or process capsicum mixture until smooth. Return to same pan, add cream; bring to the boil. Reduce heat; simmer, uncovered, 5 minutes. Serve pork with sauce.

preparation time 15 minutes **cooking time** 15 minutes **serves** 4
nutritional count per serving 19.4g total fat (10.5g saturated fat); 1404kJ (336 cal); 4.7g carbohydrate; 35g protein; 1.8g fibre

Spiced steaks with dhal

1½ teaspoons ground cumin
1 tablespoon ground coriander
2 teaspoons hot paprika
2cm piece fresh ginger (10g), grated
2 tablespoons vegetable oil
1kg beef rump steaks
1 lime, cut into wedges
⅔ cup loosely packed fresh coriander leaves
dhal
1 tablespoon vegetable oil
1 medium brown onion (150g), chopped finely
4 cloves garlic, crushed
1cm piece fresh ginger (5g), grated
1 teaspoon ground cumin
1 teaspoon ground turmeric
1 litre (4 cups) water
2 medium tomatoes (300g), chopped coarsely
1½ cups (300g) red lentils
¼ cup coarsely chopped fresh coriander

1 Make dhal.
2 Preheat grill.
3 Combine spices, ginger and oil in large bowl with beef.
4 Cook beef, under hot grill, turning once, until cooked as desired.
Cover beef; stand 5 minutes, slice thickly.
5 Serve beef with dhal, lime wedges and coriander leaves.
dhal heat oil in large heavy-based saucepan; cook onion, garlic and
ginger, stirring, until onion softens. Stir in spices; cook, stirring, until
fragrant. Add the water, tomato and lentils; bring to the boil. Reduce heat;
simmer, uncovered, about 30 minutes or until lentils are tender, stirring
occasionally. Stir in coriander.

preparation time 10 minutes **cooking time** 35 minutes **serves** 4
nutritional count per serving 32.3g total fat (9.5g saturated fat);
3143kJ (752 cal); 32.8g carbohydrate; 76g protein; 12.8g fibre

Bacon and cheese potatoes

6 large potatoes (1.8kg)
1 medium brown onion (150g), sliced thinly
3 rashers rindless bacon (195g), chopped coarsely
⅓ cup (80g) sour cream
⅓ cup (40g) grated cheddar cheese
1 tablespoon coarsely grated cheddar cheese, extra
2 teaspoons finely chopped fresh chives

1 Boil unpeeled potatoes until tender; drain.
2 Cook onion and bacon in heated oiled frying pan until browned.
3 Preheat grill.
4 Cut and discard shallow slice from each potato. Scoop two-thirds of potato from each shell; place shells on baking-paper-lined oven tray. Discard half the potato flesh; combine remainder in bowl with bacon mixture, sour cream and cheese. Spoon mixture into shells; top with extra cheese. Grill until cheese browns. Sprinkle with chives.

preparation time 20 minutes **cooking time** 30 minutes **serves** 6
nutritional count per serving 11.2g total fat (6.4g saturated fat);
1275kJ (305 cal); 35g carbohydrate; 12.5g protein; 5.4g fibre

Warm potato and kumara salad

750g kipfler potatoes, halved lengthways
500g kumara, chopped coarsely
⅓ cup (80ml) olive oil
1 small red onion (100g), sliced thinly
¼ cup finely chopped fresh dill
¼ cup finely chopped fresh basil
¼ cup (60ml) lemon juice
2 tablespoons drained capers, rinsed, chopped finely
1 tablespoon wholegrain mustard
1 clove garlic, crushed

1 Boil, steam or microwave potato and kumara, separately, until tender; drain.
2 Preheat grill.
3 Place potato and kumara, in single layer, on oiled oven trays. Brush potato and kumara with a little of the oil; grill, in batches, until browned.
4 Meanwhile, combine remaining oil, onion, dill, basil, juice, capers, mustard and garlic in large bowl. Add potato and kumara; mix gently.

preparation time 20 minutes **cooking time** 30 minutes **serves** 4
nutritional count per serving 18.7g total fat (2.6g saturated fat); 1605kJ (384 cal); 42.8g carbohydrate; 7.3g protein; 6.5g fibre

Mediterranean smash

1kg new potatoes
⅓ cup (80ml) olive oil
½ cup shredded fresh basil
3 cloves garlic, crushed
⅓ cup (55g) seeded kalamata olives, sliced

1 Preheat grill.
2 Boil unpeeled potatoes until tender; drain. Place on an oven tray; grill until browned.
3 Combine oil, half of the basil and garlic in small saucepan; cook over low heat 15 minutes.
4 Smash potatoes in large bowl with strained basil oil. Stir in olives and remaining basil.

preparation time 15 minutes **cooking time** 30 minutes **serves** 6
nutritional count per serving 12.4g total fat (1.7g saturated fat); 953kJ (228 cal); 23.3g carbohydrate; 4g protein; 3.2g fibre

Potatoes byron

1kg potatoes
300ml cream
60g butter
4 spring onions, sliced thinly
½ cup (40g) finely grated parmesan cheese

1 Oil six shallow 1-cup (250ml) pie dishes.
2 Boil potatoes until tender; drain.
3 Preheat grill.
4 Mash potato in large bowl with cream, butter and onion. Divide potato among dishes; sprinkle with cheese. Grill about 5 minutes or until browned.

preparation time 10 minutes **cooking time** 20 minutes **serves** 6
nutritional count per serving 32.3g total fat (21.2g saturated fat); 1764kJ (422 cal); 23.8g carbohydrate; 7.8g protein; 3.5g fibre

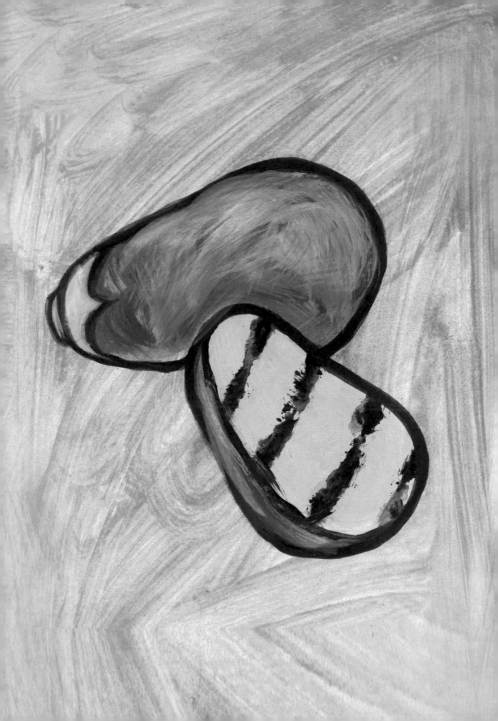

the grill pan

Seared salmon kerala-style with lime pickle yogurt

2 teaspoons coriander seeds
1 teaspoon cumin seeds
2 cardamom pods, bruised
1 cinnamon stick
1 teaspoon ground turmeric
½ teaspoon chilli powder
2 tablespoons peanut oil
2 cloves garlic, crushed
4 x 265g salmon cutlets
100g baby spinach leaves
lime pickle yogurt
½ cup (140g) yogurt
2 tablespoons lime pickle, chopped finely

1 Dry-fry coriander, cumin, cardamom and cinnamon in small heated frying pan, stirring, over medium heat until fragrant. Stir in turmeric and chilli powder; remove from heat.
2 Crush spices, using mortar and pestle, until ground finely; transfer to large bowl. Stir in oil and garlic, add fish; turn fish to coat in marinade. Cover; refrigerate 30 minutes.
3 Meanwhile, make lime pickle yogurt.
4 Cook fish in heated oiled grill pan. Serve fish with spinach and yogurt.
lime pickle yogurt combine ingredients in small bowl.

preparation time 20 minutes
cooking time 15 minutes (plus refrigeration time) **serves** 4
nutritional count per serving 29.3g total fat (6.7g saturated fat); 2082kJ (498 cal); 3.9g carbohydrate; 54.1g protein; 1.1g fibre
tip lime pickle is a mixed pickle condiment of limes that adds a hot spicy taste to meals; use sparingly. Available from Indian food stores.

Char-grilled chilli squid and rice noodle salad

800g cleaned squid hoods
450g fresh wide rice noodles
1 medium red capsicum (200g), sliced thinly
150g snow peas, trimmed, halved
1 lebanese cucumber (130g), seeded, sliced thinly
1 small red onion (100g), sliced thinly
1 cup loosely packed fresh coriander leaves
⅓ cup coarsely chopped fresh mint
sweet chilli dressing
½ cup (125ml) water
⅓ cup (75g) caster sugar
1 tablespoon white vinegar
2 fresh small red thai chillies, chopped finely

1 Cut squid down centre to open out; score the inside in a diagonal pattern. Halve squid lengthways; cut squid into 3cm pieces.
2 Make sweet chilli dressing.
3 Cook squid in heated oiled grill pan, in batches, until tender and browned.
4 Place noodles in large heatproof bowl, cover with boiling water; separate with fork, drain.
5 Place noodles in large serving bowl with squid, dressing and remaining ingredients; toss gently to combine.
sweet chilli dressing stir the water and sugar in small saucepan, over low heat, until sugar dissolves; bring to the boil. Reduce heat; simmer, uncovered, without stirring, about 5 minutes or until syrup thickens slightly. Stir in vinegar and chilli off the heat.

preparation time 15 minutes **cooking time** 15 minutes **serves** 4
nutritional count per serving 3.1g total fat (0.8g saturated fat);
1584kJ (379 cal); 48.3g carbohydrate; 38.1g protein; 2.8g fibre

Squid and watercress salad

1kg squid hoods
1½ teaspoons ground cumin
2 tablespoons finely chopped fresh dill
2 tablespoons lemon juice
2 tablespoons barbecue sauce
¼ cup (60ml) sweet chilli sauce
¼ cup (60ml) peanut oil
1 tablespoon finely grated lemon rind
2 cloves garlic, crushed
2 lebanese cucumbers (260g)
1 medium red capsicum (200g), sliced thinly
140g watercress
1 tablespoon water

1 Cut squid in half lengthways, score inside surface of each piece; cut diagonally into 2cm-wide strips.
2 Combine cumin, dill, juice, sauces and oil in small jug; mix well.
3 Combine squid, rind and garlic in large bowl with half of the cumin mixture; cover, refrigerate at least 20 minutes or until required. Cover remaining cumin mixture; refrigerate until required.
4 Drain squid; discard marinade. Cook squid in heated oiled grill pan until just cooked; cover to keep warm.
5 Halve cucumbers lengthways; cut into thin slices. Combine cucumber in large bowl with capsicum and watercress.
6 Stir the water into reserved cumin mixture, pour over salad; toss gently to combine. Serve squid with salad.

preparation time 30 minutes (plus refrigeration time)
cooking time 10 minutes **serves** 4
nutritional count per serving 17.4g total fat (3.6g saturated fat); 1626kJ (389 cal); 11.7g carbohydrate; 44.2g protein; 3.7g fibre

Char-grilled octopus salad

1 fresh long red chilli, chopped finely
1 teaspoon finely grated lime rind
1 teaspoon salt
2 tablespoons rice flour
1kg cleaned octopus, quartered
200g mizuna
150g snow peas, sliced thinly
chilli lime dressing
1 fresh small red thai chilli, chopped finely
1 teaspoon finely grated lime rind
2 tablespoons lime juice
1 tablespoon peanut oil
2cm piece fresh ginger (10g), grated

1 Combine chilli, rind, salt and flour in large bowl with octopus.
2 Cook octopus mixture in heated oiled grill pan until tender.
3 Make chilli lime dressing.
4 Place remaining ingredients in large bowl with octopus and dressing; toss gently to combine.
chilli lime dressing place ingredients in screw-top jar; shake well.

preparation time 20 minutes **cooking time** 20 minutes **serves** 4
nutritional count per serving 9.4g total fat (1.8g saturated fat);
1668kJ (399 cal); 10.5g carbohydrate; 65.8g protein; 2.2g fibre

Grilled tuna with japanese chilled soba salad

250g soba noodles
¼ cup (70g) pickled pink ginger, sliced thinly
4 green onions, sliced thinly
4 x 175g tuna steaks
1 sheet toasted nori, shredded
soy mirin dressing
¼ cup (60ml) light soy sauce
⅓ cup (80ml) mirin
1 tablespoon rice vinegar
2 tablespoons cooking sake
1 teaspoon sesame oil
1 teaspoon wasabi paste

1 Cook noodles in large saucepan of boiling water, uncovered, until tender; drain. Rinse under cold water, drain thoroughly.
2 Make soy mirin dressing.
3 Place cold noodles, ginger and onion in large bowl with three-quarters of the dressing; toss gently to combine. Cover; refrigerate until chilled.
4 Cook tuna, both sides, in heated oiled grill pan until just cooked (do not overcook or tuna will dry out).
5 Serve tuna drizzled with remaining dressing, topped with nori. Serve with soba salad.
soy mirin dressing place ingredients in screw-top jar; shake well.

preparation time 20 minutes
cooking time 10 minutes (plus refrigeration time) **serves** 4
nutritional count per serving 11.9g total fat (4.3g saturated fat); 2207kJ (528 cal); 45.1g carbohydrate; 52.1g protein; 2.8g fibre

Herbed fish skewers with potato smash and skordalia

You need to soak eight bamboo skewers in cold water for at least an hour before use to prevent them from splintering or burning during cooking.

800g white fish fillets, cut into 2cm pieces
¼ cup (60ml) olive oil
2 tablespoons finely chopped fresh flat-leaf parsley
2 tablespoons finely chopped fresh lemon thyme
1kg new potatoes, unpeeled
½ cup (120g) sour cream
40g butter, softened
skordalia
1 small potato (120g)
1 slice white bread
2 cloves garlic, crushed
1 tablespoon apple cider vinegar
¼ cup (60ml) water
2 tablespoons olive oil

1 Thread fish onto skewers; place in medium shallow dish. Brush with combined oil and herbs. Cover; refrigerate 20 minutes.
2 Meanwhile, make skordalia.
3 Boil, steam or microwave potatoes until tender; drain. Mash half the potatoes in medium bowl with sour cream and butter until smooth. Using fork, crush remaining potatoes until skins burst; fold into mash mixture. Cover to keep warm.
4 Cook skewers in heated oiled grill pan; serve with smash and skordalia.
skordalia boil, steam or microwave potato until tender; drain. Mash potato in medium bowl until smooth. Discard crusts from bread. Soak bread in small bowl of cold water; drain. Squeeze out excess water. Blend or process bread with remaining ingredients until smooth. Stir bread mixture into potato.

preparation time 20 minutes (plus refrigeration time)
cooking time 30 minutes **serves** 4
nutritional count per serving 44.7g total fat (16.7g saturated fat); 3114kJ (745 cal); 39.8g carbohydrate; 42.9g protein; 5.3g fibre
tip we used blue-eye in this recipe, but you can use any firm white fish.

Scallop and fish skewers with tomato salsa

You need to soak 12 bamboo skewers in cold water for at least an hour before use to prevent them from splintering or burning during cooking.

500g white fish fillets, cut into 2cm pieces
500g scallops, roe removed
1/3 cup finely chopped fresh basil
1/4 cup (60ml) red wine vinegar
2 tablespoons olive oil
1 teaspoon cracked black pepper
3 large egg tomatoes (270g), cut into 1cm pieces
250g yellow teardrop tomatoes, halved
250g cherry tomatoes, halved
1/2 cup loosely packed fresh basil leaves, torn
red wine vinaigrette
2 tablespoons red wine vinegar
1/4 cup (60ml) olive oil
1 teaspoon dijon mustard
1 teaspoon caster sugar

1 Thread fish and scallops, alternately, onto skewers; place in large shallow dish, drizzle with combined chopped basil, vinegar, oil and pepper.
2 Make red wine vinaigrette.
3 Cook skewers on heated oiled grill pan until cooked as desired.
4 Meanwhile, place tomatoes, torn basil and vinaigrette in medium bowl; toss gently to combine. Serve salad with skewers.
red wine vinaigrette place ingredients in screw-top jar; shake well.

preparation time 30 minutes **cooking time** 10 minutes **serves** 4
nutritional count per serving 26.7g total fat (4.3g saturated fat); 1827kJ (437 cal); 6.4g carbohydrate; 41.6g protein; 3.5g fibre
tip we used blue-eye in this recipe, but you can use any firm white fish.

Fish fillets with tomato, caper and walnut dressing

4 x 185g white fish fillets
tomato, caper and walnut dressing
250g cherry tomatoes
60g butter
1 tablespoon finely grated lemon rind
2 teaspoons lemon juice
1 teaspoon drained capers, rinsed, chopped finely
¼ cup (30g) finely chopped walnuts
½ cup coarsely chopped fresh flat-leaf parsley

1 Make tomato, caper and walnut dressing.
2 Cook fish in heated oiled grill pan until cooked as desired.
3 Serve fish topped with dressing.
tomato, caper and walnut dressing   cook tomatoes in heated oiled grill pan until tender. Melt butter in small saucepan; add tomatoes and remaining ingredients, stirring until hot.

preparation time 15 minutes   **cooking time** 20 minutes   **serves** 4
nutritional count per serving   19.8g total fat (9.2g saturated fat);
1471kJ (352 cal); 2g carbohydrate; 40.1g protein; 1.9g fibre
tip we used barramundi in this recipe, but you can use any firm white fish.

Seafood in lemon cream sauce

500g uncooked medium king prawns
250g scallops, roe removed
2 teaspoons olive oil
3 cloves garlic, crushed
340g asparagus, halved crossways
150g sugar snap peas, trimmed
2 teaspoons lemon juice
2 tablespoons dry white wine
¾ cup (180ml) cream
2 tablespoons coarsely chopped fresh flat-leaf parsley

1 Shell and devein prawns, leaving tails intact; combine with scallops, oil and garlic in medium bowl.
2 Cook seafood in heated oiled grill pan until changed in colour. Remove from heat; cover to keep warm.
3 Meanwhile, boil, steam or microwave asparagus and peas, separately, until tender. Drain; cover to keep warm.
4 Simmer juice and wine in small saucepan, uncovered, about 1 minute or until reduced by half. Add cream; bring to the boil. Reduce heat; simmer, uncovered, 2 minutes. Add seafood; simmer, uncovered, until hot.
5 Serve seafood with vegetables, sprinkled with chopped parsley.

preparation time 15 minutes **cooking time** 10 minutes **serves** 4
nutritional count per serving 22.7g total fat (13.4g saturated fat); 1367kJ (327 cal); 4.6g carbohydrate; 23.7g protein; 2.2g fibre

Smoked trout and potato salad

750g new potatoes, halved
2 x 385g whole smoked trout
2 tablespoons lemon juice
1 tablespoon olive oil
1 teaspoon dijon mustard
1 small red onion (100g), sliced thinly
2 green onions, sliced thinly
2 tablespoons drained capers, rinsed
1 tablespoon finely chopped fresh dill
4 large iceberg lettuce leaves

1 Boil, steam or microwave potato until tender; drain. Cook potato in heated oiled grill pan until browned both sides.
2 Meanwhile, discard skin and bones from fish; flake flesh into large bowl.
3 Place juice, oil and mustard in screw-top jar; shake well.
4 Combine potato, dressing, onions, capers and dill in bowl with trout; divide salad among lettuce leaves.

preparation time 5 minutes **cooking time** 25 minutes **serves** 4
nutritional count per serving 16.6g total fat (1.9g saturated fat);
1404kJ (336 cal); 27.6g carbohydrate; 31.2g protein; 4.8g fibre

Warm lemon-herbed pasta and fresh salmon salad

1 cup (120g) frozen peas
170g asparagus, trimmed, chopped coarsely
500g piece salmon fillet
625g spinach and ricotta agnolotti pasta
½ cup fresh flat-leaf parsley leaves
1 tablespoon water
¼ cup (60ml) olive oil
1 teaspoon finely grated lemon rind
¼ cup (60ml) lemon juice

1 Boil, steam or microwave peas and asparagus, separately, until just tender; drain. Rinse under cold water; drain.
2 Cook salmon in heated oiled grill pan until browned both sides and cooked as desired. Place salmon in large bowl then, using fork, flake into chunks.
3 Meanwhile, cook pasta in large saucepan of boiling water, uncovered, until just tender; drain. Add to salmon.
4 Combine parsley, the water, oil, rind and juice in small jug; pour over salmon and pasta. Add peas and asparagus; toss gently to combine.

preparation time 15 minutes **cooking time** 20 minutes **serves** 4
nutritional count per serving 33.7g total fat (10.6g saturated fat); 2428kJ (581 cal); 26.9g carbohydrate; 39.8g protein; 5.5g fibre
tip fresh spinach and ricotta agnolotti is found in most supermarkets' refrigerated sections. You can substitute ravioli or tortellini for the agnolotti, but none should contain meat or poultry in their filling.

Grilled salmon with nam jim and herb salad

4 x 220g salmon fillets, skin-on
nam jim
3 long green chillies, chopped coarsely
2 fresh small red thai chillies, chopped coarsely
2 cloves garlic, quartered
1 shallot (25g), quartered
2cm piece fresh ginger (10g), quartered
⅓ cup (80ml) lime juice
2 tablespoons fish sauce
1 tablespoon grated palm sugar
1 tablespoon peanut oil
¼ cup (35g) roasted unsalted cashews, chopped finely
herb salad
1½ cups loosely packed fresh mint leaves
1 cup loosely packed fresh coriander leaves
1 cup loosely packed fresh basil leaves, torn
1 medium red onion (170g), sliced thinly
2 lebanese cucumbers (260g), seeded, sliced thinly

1 Make nam jim.
2 Cook salmon, both sides, in heated oiled grill pan until cooked as desired.
3 Meanwhile, make herb salad.
4 Serve salmon and herb salad topped with nam jim.
nam jim blend or process chillies, garlic, shallot, ginger, juice, sauce, sugar and oil until smooth; stir in nuts.
herb salad combine ingredients in medium bowl.

preparation time 30 minutes **cooking time** 10 minutes **serves** 4
nutritional count per serving 25g total fat (5.1g saturated fat); 1948kJ (466 cal); 10.8g carbohydrate; 47.6g protein; 4.4g fibre

Char-grilled salmon with avocado salsa

4 x 200g salmon fillets
1 large avocado (320g), sliced thickly
1 small red onion (100g), sliced thinly
2 tablespoons coarsely chopped fresh dill
2 tablespoons drained baby capers, rinsed
¼ cup (60ml) lemon juice
¼ cup (60ml) olive oil
75g baby rocket leaves

1 Cook salmon in heated oiled grill pan.
2 Meanwhile, combine avocado, onion, dill and capers in medium bowl.
3 Place juice and oil in screw-top jar; shake well.
4 Serve salmon on rocket with avocado salsa; drizzle with dressing.

preparation time 15 minutes **cooking time** 10 minutes **serves** 4
nutritional count per serving 46.7g total fat (6.9g saturated fat);
2261kJ (541 cal); 3g carbohydrate; 41g protein; 1.6g fibre

Teriyaki salmon with soba salad

250g dried soba noodles
4 x 200g salmon fillets
¼ cup (60ml) teriyaki sauce
2 tablespoons sweet chilli sauce
1 medium red capsicum (200g), sliced thinly
4 green onions, sliced thinly
1 tablespoon light soy sauce
2 teaspoons lime juice
1 teaspoon sesame oil

1 Cook noodles in large saucepan of boiling water, uncovered, until just tender; drain. Rinse under cold water; drain.
2 Meanwhile, combine salmon, teriyaki sauce, and 1 tablespoon of the sweet chilli sauce in medium bowl.
3 Cook salmon in heated oiled grill pan, brushing occasionally with teriyaki mixture, until cooked as desired.
4 Combine noodles with remaining ingredients in large bowl. Serve soba salad with salmon, and lime wedges, if desired.

preparation time 10 minutes **cooking time** 15 minutes **serves** 4
nutritional count per serving 16.4g total fat (3.5g saturated fat); 2249kJ (538 cal); 47.4g carbohydrate; 48g protein; 3.2g fibre

Fish fillets with walnut gremolata

4 medium potatoes (800g), quartered
40g butter, chopped coarsely
¼ cup (60ml) milk
1 clove garlic, crushed
4 x 200g white fish fillets
1 tablespoon olive oil
walnut gremolata
⅓ cup (35g) walnuts, roasted, chopped finely
2 tablespoons finely chopped lemon rind
¼ cup finely chopped fresh flat-leaf parsley
1 clove garlic, crushed

1 Make walnut gremolata.
2 Boil, steam or microwave potato until tender; drain. Mash potato with butter, milk and garlic.
3 Brush fish with oil; cook in heated oiled grill pan until browned both sides and just cooked.
4 Serve fish with garlic mash; sprinkle with gremolata.
walnut gremolata   combine ingredients in small bowl; cover until required.

preparation time 15 minutes   **cooking time** 15 minutes   **serves** 4
nutritional count per serving   24g total fat (8.2g saturated fat);
2098kJ (502 cal); 22.5g carbohydrate; 46.7g protein; 3.8g fibre
tip   we used bream in this recipe, but you can use any firm white fish.

Balmain bugs with oregano

16 uncooked medium balmain bugs (3.2kg), halved, cleaned
¼ cup (60ml) dry white wine
¼ cup (60ml) lime juice
¼ cup (60ml) olive oil
2 cloves garlic, crushed
2 tablespoons finely chopped fresh oregano

1 Combine bugs with remaining ingredients in large bowl. Cover;
refrigerate at least 20 minutes or until required.
2 Drain bugs over small bowl; reserve marinade. Cook bugs in heated
oiled grill pan, brushing occasionally with reserved marinade, until just
changed in colour.
3 Serve bugs sprinkled with extra chopped fresh oregano, if desired.

preparation time 25 minutes (plus refrigeration time)
cooking time 10 minutes **serves** 4
nutritional count per serving 15.9g total fat (2.4g saturated fat);
1542kJ (369 cal); 0.4g carbohydrate; 53g protein; 0.3g fibre
tip we used balmain bugs in this recipe, but you could also use the same
weight of scampi or uncooked large king prawns.

Fish fillets with fennel and onion salad

1 medium red onion (170g), sliced thinly
4 green onions, sliced thinly
1 large fennel (550g), trimmed, sliced thinly
2 trimmed celery stalks (200g), sliced thinly
½ cup coarsely chopped fresh flat-leaf parsley
⅓ cup (80ml) orange juice
¼ cup (60ml) olive oil
2 cloves garlic, crushed
2 teaspoons sambal oelek
4 x 275g white fish fillets, with skin on

1 Combine onions, fennel, celery and parsley in medium bowl.
2 Place juice, oil, garlic and sambal in screw-top jar; shake well.
3 Cook fish in heated oiled grill pan until browned both sides and just cooked.
4 Pour half the dressing over salad in bowl; toss gently to combine. Serve salad topped with fish; drizzle with remaining dressing.

preparation time 15 minutes **cooking time** 10 minutes **serves** 4
nutritional count per serving 20g total fat (3.9g saturated fat); 1902kJ (455 cal); 8.4g carbohydrate; 58.2g protein; 4.4g fibre
tip we used snapper in this recipe, but you can use any firm white fish.

Tuna with kipfler mash and salsa verde

1kg kipfler potatoes, peeled, halved
30g butter
1 tablespoon olive oil
4 x 175g tuna steaks
80g baby rocket leaves
salsa verde
½ cup firmly packed fresh flat-leaf parsley leaves
¼ cup firmly packed fresh mint leaves
⅔ cup (160ml) olive oil
¼ cup (50g) drained capers, rinsed
2 teaspoons dijon mustard
2 tablespoons lemon juice
8 drained anchovy fillets
1 clove garlic, quartered

1 Boil, steam or microwave potato until tender; drain. Using potato masher, crush potato roughly in large bowl with butter and oil. Cover to keep warm.
2 Meanwhile, make salsa verde.
3 Cook tuna in heated oiled grill pan until just cooked (do not overcook or tuna will dry out).
4 Divide rocket and potato among serving plates; top with tuna, drizzle with salsa verde.
salsa verde blend or process ingredients until just combined. Transfer to medium jug; whisk before pouring over fish.

preparation time 20 minutes **cooking time** 15 minutes **serves** 4
nutritional count per serving 58.3g total fat (14g saturated fat); 3570kJ (854 cal); 28.5g carbohydrate; 51.8g protein; 4.5g fibre

Spicy sardines with orange and olive salad

24 butterflied sardines (1kg)
1 clove garlic, crushed
1 tablespoon olive oil
2 tablespoons orange juice
1 teaspoon hot paprika
1 teaspoon finely chopped fresh oregano
orange and olive salad
2 medium oranges (480g)
⅓ cup (40g) seeded black olives, chopped coarsely
50g baby rocket leaves
1 fresh long red chilli, sliced thinly
1 tablespoon orange juice
½ teaspoon finely chopped fresh oregano
1 tablespoon olive oil

1 Combine sardines and remaining ingredients in medium bowl.
2 Make orange and olive salad.
3 Cook sardines, in batches, in heated oiled grill pan until browned both sides and cooked through.
4 Divide sardines among plates; serve with salad.
orange and olive salad peel then segment oranges over medium bowl, add remaining ingredients; toss gently to combine.

preparation time 20 minutes **cooking time** 15 minutes **serves** 4
nutritional count per serving 36.2g total fat (8.3g saturated fat);
2500kJ (598 cal); 11.5g carbohydrate; 56g protein; 2.2g fibre
tip sardines are available already butterflied from most fishmongers.

Sardines with tomatoes and caper dressing

12 whole sardines (450g)
4 medium egg tomatoes (300g), sliced thickly
1 small red onion (100g), sliced thinly
caper dressing
⅓ cup (80ml) red wine vinegar
¼ cup (60ml) olive oil
1 tablespoon drained baby capers, rinsed
1 clove garlic, crushed
2 tablespoons coarsely chopped fresh flat-leaf parsley

1 Remove and discard sardine heads. To butterfly sardines, cut through the underside of fish to the tail. Break backbone at the tail; peel away backbone, trim fish.
2 Cook sardines in heated oiled grill pan until browned both sides and just cooked.
3 Meanwhile, make caper dressing.
4 Serve sardines with tomato and onion; spoon over caper dressing.
caper dressing place ingredients in screw-top jar; shake well.

preparation time 25 minutes **cooking time** 10 minutes **serves** 4
nutritional count per serving 16.3g total fat (2.7g saturated fat);
1091kJ (261 cal); 3.2g carbohydrate; 24.2g protein; 1.5g fibre
tip sardines are available already butterflied from most fishmongers.

Prawn kebabs with chilli lime sauce

You need to soak eight bamboo skewers in cold water for at least an hour before use to prevent them from splintering or burning during cooking.

32 uncooked medium prawns (1.4kg)
10cm stick fresh lemon grass (20g), chopped finely
2 cloves garlic, crushed
1 tablespoon balsamic vinegar
1 tablespoon coarsely chopped fresh coriander
1 tablespoon peanut oil
4 green onions, cut into 5cm lengths
chilli lime sauce
⅔ cup (150g) white sugar
½ cup (125ml) water
1 teaspoon finely grated lime rind
2 fresh small red thai chillies, chopped finely
2 tablespoons sweet chilli sauce
⅓ cup (80ml) lime juice

1 Shell and devein prawns, leaving tails intact. Combine lemon grass, garlic, vinegar, coriander and oil in medium bowl with prawns. Cover; refrigerate at least 20 minutes or until required.
2 Meanwhile, make chilli lime sauce.
3 Drain prawns; discard marinade. Thread prawns and onion onto skewers. Cook in heated oiled grill pan until browned both sides. Serve kebabs with sauce.
chilli lime sauce stir sugar and the water in small saucepan over heat, without boiling, until sugar dissolves. Simmer, without stirring, 5 minutes. Add rind, chilli and sauce; simmer, 5 minutes. Stir in juice; cool.

preparation time 25 minutes (plus refrigeration time)
cooking time 20 minutes **serves** 4
nutritional count per serving 5.5g total fat (1g saturated fat); 1233kJ (295 cal); 40.3g carbohydrate; 21.1g protein; 1g fibre

Fish steaks with roasted mediterranean vegetables

1 medium red capsicum (200g), sliced thickly
1 medium yellow capsicum (200g), sliced thickly
1 medium eggplant (300g), sliced thickly
2 large zucchini (300g), sliced thickly
½ cup (125ml) olive oil
250g cherry tomatoes
¼ cup (60ml) balsamic vinegar
1 clove garlic, crushed
2 teaspoons white sugar
4 x 220g white fish steaks
¼ cup coarsely chopped fresh basil

1 Preheat oven to 220°C/200°C fan-forced.
2 Combine capsicums, eggplant and zucchini with 2 tablespoons of the oil in large baking dish; roast 15 minutes. Add tomatoes; roast about 5 minutes or until vegetables are just tender.
3 Meanwhile, place vinegar, garlic, sugar and remaining oil in screw-top jar; shake well.
4 Brush a third of the dressing over fish; cook, both sides, in heated oiled grill pan until just cooked.
5 Combine vegetables in large bowl with basil and remaining dressing; toss gently to combine. Divide vegetables among serving plates; top with fish.

preparation time 25 minutes **cooking time** 30 minutes **serves** 4
nutritional count per serving 33.9g total fat (5.6g saturated fat); 2274kJ (544 cal); 9.3g carbohydrate; 48.2g protein; 4.8g fibre
tip we used swordfish in this recipe, but you can use any firm white fish.

Chicken quesadillas with jalapeño tomato salsa

2 teaspoons mexican chilli powder
2 medium avocados (500g)
¼ cup (60g) sour cream
2 tablespoons lime juice
2 tablespoons vegetable oil
2 teaspoons ground cumin
2 teaspoons ground coriander
1kg chicken tenderloins
8 large flour tortillas (320g)
1 cup (120g) coarsely grated cheddar cheese
jalapeño tomato salsa
4 medium egg tomatoes (300g), seeded, chopped finely
¼ cup (60g) bottled jalapeño chillies, rinsed, drained, chopped finely
¼ cup coarsely chopped fresh coriander
1 medium avocado (250g), chopped coarsely
1 tablespoon lime juice

1 Preheat grill.
2 Place chilli powder, avocados, sour cream and juice in medium bowl; mash roughly with fork.
3 Combine oil and spices in large bowl with chicken. Cook chicken in heated oiled grill pan, in batches, until cooked.
4 Meanwhile, make jalapeño tomato salsa.
5 Divide chicken and avocado mixture among tortillas; fold to enclose filling. Place quesadillas on oven tray; sprinkle with cheese. Grill until cheese melts and is golden brown. Serve quesadillas with salsa.
jalapeño tomato salsa combine ingredients in medium bowl.

preparation time 20 minutes **cooking time** 15 minutes **serves 4**
nutritional count per serving 81g total fat (25.3g saturated fat); 4937kJ (1181 cal); 44.9g carbohydrate; 66.3g protein; 5.5g fibre

Grilled turkey steaks with green olive and tomato relish

1kg potatoes
4 turkey steaks (800g)
1 teaspoon sea salt
½ teaspoon cracked black pepper
green olive and tomato relish
1 tablespoon extra virgin olive oil
1 small red onion (100g), chopped finely
1 clove garlic, crushed
2 large green tomatoes (440g), chopped finely
2 cups (240g) seeded green olives, chopped finely
2 tablespoons white sugar
¼ cup (60ml) apple cider vinegar
2 tablespoons drained capers, rinsed, chopped finely
⅓ cup finely chopped fresh flat-leaf parsley

1 Make green olive and tomato relish.
2 Meanwhile, cut potatoes into 1cm slices; cook in heated oiled grill pan, uncovered, until tender.
3 Sprinkle turkey with salt and pepper; cook in same grill pan until cooked through. Serve with potato and relish.
green olive and tomato relish heat oil in medium saucepan; cook onion and garlic, stirring, until onion softens. Add tomato, olives, sugar and vinegar; cook, stirring occasionally, 10 minutes. Remove from heat; stir in capers and parsley.

preparation time 10 minutes **cooking time** 30 minutes **serves** 4
nutritional count per serving 15.7g total fat (3.2g saturated fat); 217kJ (520 cal); 41.6g carbohydrate; 48.4g protein; 8.0g fibre
tip store the relish, covered, in the refrigerator for up to two weeks.

Maple-glazed chicken and kumara skewers with spinach pecan salad

1 large kumara (500g), cut into 2cm pieces
660g chicken thigh fillets, cut into 3cm pieces
12 shallots (300g), halved
2 tablespoons maple syrup
1 tablespoon apple cider vinegar
1 teaspoon dijon mustard
spinach pecan salad
2 tablespoons maple syrup
1 tablespoon apple cider vinegar
1 teaspoon dijon mustard
200g yellow grape tomatoes, halved
1 cup (120g) roasted pecans
80g baby spinach leaves, trimmed
½ small red onion (50g), sliced thinly

1 Boil, steam or microwave kumara until tender; drain. Thread kumara, chicken and shallot, alternately, onto skewers.
2 Combine syrup, vinegar and mustard in small bowl.
3 Cook skewers in heated oiled grill pan, covered with foil, 10 minutes. Uncover, brush skewers all over with syrup mixture. Turn; cook, brushing occasionally with syrup mixture, about 5 minutes or until chicken is cooked through.
4 Meanwhile, make spinach pecan salad.
5 Serve skewers with salad.
spinach pecan salad whisk syrup, vinegar and mustard in large bowl, add tomatoes, pecans, spinach leaves and onion; toss gently to combine.

preparation time 25 minutes **cooking time** 20 minutes **serves** 4
nutritional count per serving 35g total fat (5g saturated fat);
2650kJ (634 cal); 39.5g carbohydrate; 38g protein; 7g fibre
tip if using bamboo skewers, you need to soak them in cold water for at least an hour before use to prevent them from splintering or burning during cooking.

Chicken yakitori with sesame dipping sauce

You need to soak 12 bamboo skewers in cold water for at least an hour before use to prevent them from splintering or burning during cooking.

12 chicken tenderloins (1kg)
sesame dipping sauce
¼ cup (60ml) light soy sauce
2 tablespoons mirin
3 teaspoons white sugar
½ teaspoon sesame oil
1 teaspoon sesame seeds

1 Make sesame dipping sauce.
2 Thread each tenderloin onto a skewer; brush skewers with half the dipping sauce.
3 Cook skewers, in batches, in heated oiled grill pan until chicken is cooked. Serve skewers with remaining dipping sauce.
sesame dipping sauce stir ingredients in small saucepan over medium heat until sugar dissolves.

preparation time 20 minutes **cooking time** 10 minutes **serves** 4
nutritional count per serving 20.4g total fat (6.4g saturated fat);
1643kJ (393 cal); 3.8g carbohydrate; 47.1g protein; 0.1g fibre

Portuguese-style chicken

3 fresh small red thai chillies, chopped finely
2 teaspoons dried chilli flakes
3 cloves garlic, crushed
¼ cup (60ml) apple cider vinegar
2 teaspoons finely grated lemon rind
⅔ cup (160ml) lemon juice
2 teaspoons smoked paprika
½ cup finely chopped fresh flat-leaf parsley
2 teaspoons coarse cooking salt
¼ teaspoon cracked black pepper
2 tablespoons olive oil
4 chicken marylands (1.4kg)
80g mesclun

1 Combine chillies, garlic, vinegar, rind, juice, paprika, parsley, salt, pepper and oil in large bowl with chicken. Cover; refrigerate overnight.
2 Cook chicken, covered, in heated oiled grill pan over medium heat, about 45 minutes or until cooked through.
3 Serve chicken with mesclun, and lemon wedges, if desired.

preparation time 15 minutes (plus refrigeration time)
cooking time 45 minutes **serves** 4
nutritional count per serving 41.8g total fat (11.7g saturated fat); 2337kJ (559 cal); 1.5g carbohydrate; 43g protein; 1.1g fibre

Rosemary and prosciutto chicken legs with creamy risoni

8 stalks fresh rosemary
8 chicken drumsticks (1.2kg)
8 slices prosciutto (120g)
1 cup (220g) risoni
1 tablespoon olive oil
1 medium brown onion (150g), chopped finely
1 clove garlic, crushed
300ml cream
¼ teaspoon dried chilli flakes
250g cherry tomatoes, halved
1 tablespoon fresh lemon thyme leaves

1 Press one rosemary stalk onto each drumstick; firmly wrap one prosciutto slice around each to hold in place.
2 Cook chicken in heated oiled grill pan until brown all over. Cover chicken; cook about 40 minutes or until cooked.
3 Meanwhile, cook risoni in large saucepan of boiling water until just tender; drain. Rinse under cold water; drain.
4 Heat oil in large frying pan; cook onion and garlic, stirring, until onion softens. Add cream and chilli; simmer, uncovered, until mixture thickens. Add risoni, tomato and half the thyme; cook, stirring, until tomato just softens. Serve with chicken; sprinkle with remaining thyme.

preparation time 30 minutes **cooking time** 45 minutes **serves** 4
nutritional count per serving 60.4g total fat (29.2g saturated fat);
3783kJ (509 cal); 42.6g carbohydrate; 47.3g protein; 3.4g fibre

Chicken burgers italian-style

500g chicken mince
¼ cup (35g) sun-dried tomatoes, drained, chopped finely
1 tablespoon finely chopped fresh basil
1 egg
1 cup (70g) stale breadcrumbs
3 cloves garlic, crushed
4 slices pancetta (60g)
1 square loaf focaccia (440g)
½ cup (150g) mayonnaise
40g baby rocket leaves
120g bocconcini cheese, sliced thickly

1 Combine mince in large bowl with tomato, basil, egg, breadcrumbs and about a third of the garlic; shape mixture into four burgers.
2 Cook burgers in heated oiled grill pan about 30 minutes or until cooked.
3 Cook pancetta in same grill pan until crisp; drain.
4 Quarter focaccia; slice each square in half horizontally. Toast cut sides in same grill pan.
5 Combine mayonnaise with remaining garlic; spread on focaccia bases. Sandwich rocket, burgers, pancetta and cheese between focaccia pieces.

preparation time 20 minutes **cooking time** 30 minutes **serves** 4
nutritional count per serving 34.9g total fat (9.3g saturated fat); 3357kJ (803 cal); 71.5g carbohydrate; 47.6g protein; 5.6g fibre

Fontina, pancetta and sage chicken

4 x 200g chicken breast fillets
4 thin slices fontina cheese (100g)
4 slices pancetta (60g)
2 tablespoons coarsely chopped fresh sage
2 tablespoons olive oil
2 cloves garlic, crushed
16 whole sage leaves

1 Slit a pocket in one side of each fillet but do not cut all the way through. Divide cheese, pancetta and chopped sage among pockets; secure with toothpicks. Brush chicken with combined oil and garlic.
2 Cook chicken, both sides, in heated oiled grill pan, about 20 minutes or until cooked. Remove toothpicks before serving.
3 Cook whole sage leaves in grill pan until golden brown. Serve chicken topped with sage leaves.

preparation time 15 minutes **cooking time** 20 minutes **serves** 4
nutritional count per serving 23.3g total fat (8g saturated fat);
1806kJ (432 cal); 0.3g carbohydrate; 55.3g protein; 0.3g fibre

Indochine grilled chicken salad

2 teaspoons five-spice powder
¼ cup (60ml) mirin
2 tablespoons chinese cooking wine
2 cloves garlic, crushed
4 x 200g chicken thigh cutlets
125g rice vermicelli
150g snow peas, sliced thinly
1 cup (80g) bean sprouts
2 green onions, sliced thinly
½ cup coarsely chopped fresh coriander
¼ cup loosely packed fresh vietnamese mint leaves
2 medium carrots (240g), cut into matchsticks
lime dressing
⅓ cup (80ml) lime juice
⅓ cup (80ml) mirin
2 cloves garlic, crushed
1 tablespoon grated palm sugar

1 Combine five-spice, mirin, wine and garlic in large bowl with chicken.
Cover; refrigerate 3 hours or overnight.
2 Make lime dressing.
3 Cook chicken in heated oiled grill pan, turning and brushing
occasionally with marinade, about 40 minutes or until cooked.
4 Meanwhile, place vermicelli in large heatproof bowl, cover with boiling
water; stand until just tender, drain. Rinse vermicelli under cold water; drain.
5 Place vermicelli and dressing in large bowl with remaining ingredients;
toss salad to combine. Serve with chicken.
lime dressing place ingredients in screw-top jar; shake well.

preparation time 25 minutes (plus refrigeration time)
cooking time 40 minutes **serves** 4
nutritional count per serving 20.5g total fat (6.6g saturated fat);
1668kJ (399 cal); 17.2g carbohydrate; 26.9g protein; 4.2g fibre

Grilled chicken with green olive butter

400g new potatoes, sliced thickly
800g chicken breast fillets
150g baby spinach leaves
green olive butter
100g butter, softened
¾ cup (90g) seeded green olives, chopped coarsely
1 teaspoon finely grated lemon rind
1 clove garlic, crushed
1 tablespoon finely chopped fresh basil

1 Make green olive butter.
2 Boil, steam or microwave potato until tender; drain. Cover to keep warm.
3 Meanwhile, halve chicken fillets horizontally. Cook chicken in heated oiled grill pan.
4 Divide potato among plates; top with spinach, chicken then olive butter.
green olive butter combine ingredients in small bowl.

preparation time 15 minutes **cooking time** 20 minutes **serves** 4
nutritional count per serving 32g total fat (17g saturated fat);
2316kJ (554 cal); 18.6g carbohydrate; 46.5g protein; 3.5g fibre

Kofta with spiced eggplant and date chutney

¼ cup (50g) brown rice
1 tablespoon olive oil
1 small brown onion (80g), chopped finely
1 clove garlic, crushed
1 long green chilli, chopped finely
500g chicken mince
½ cup firmly packed fresh coriander leaves
1 egg
spiced eggplant
1 tablespoon olive oil
2 teaspoons cumin seeds
2 teaspoons yellow mustard seeds
6 baby eggplants (360g), sliced thickly
1 medium brown onion (150g), sliced thinly
1 clove garlic, crushed
½ cup (125ml) water
420g can chickpeas, rinsed, drained
¼ cup firmly packed fresh coriander leaves
date chutney
½ cup (70g) seeded dried dates, chopped finely
¼ cup (60ml) orange juice
¼ cup (60ml) water

1 Cook rice in large saucepan of boiling water until tender; drain. Rinse; drain.
2 Heat oil in small frying pan; cook onion, garlic and chilli, stirring, until onion softens. Process onion mixture with chicken, rice, coriander and egg until smooth; shape into 12 patties, place on tray. Cover; refrigerate.
3 Make spiced eggplant. Make date chutney.
4 Cook patties in heated oiled grill pan until browned and cooked. Serve with eggplant; top with chutney.
spiced eggplant heat oil in saucepan; fry seeds over low heat until fragrant. Add eggplant, onion and garlic; cook, stirring, 5 minutes or until soft. Add the water and chickpeas; bring to the boil. Reduce heat; simmer, 15 minutes or until thickened. Remove from heat; cool 10 minutes, stir in coriander.
date chutney bring ingredients in small saucepan to the boil. Reduce heat; simmer, uncovered, 5 minutes. Cool 5 minutes; blend or process until smooth.
preparation time 30 minutes (plus refrigeration time)
cooking time 45 minutes **serves** 4
nutritional count per serving 17.8g total fat (3.5g saturated fat); 1935kJ (463 cal); 37.1g carbohydrate; 35.4g protein; 8.6g fibre

Grilled chicken, brie and avocado on ciabatta

2 chicken breast fillets (400g)
4 thick slices ciabatta (140g)
⅓ cup (80ml) sweet chilli sauce
50g baby rocket leaves
100g brie cheese, cut into 4 slices
1 small avocado (200g), sliced thinly

1 Halve chicken pieces diagonally; slice through each piece horizontally (you will have eight pieces). Cook in heated oiled grill pan until chicken is browned both sides and cooked through.
2 Toast bread, both sides, in same grill pan.
3 Spread half the sauce over toast slices; top with rocket, chicken, cheese then avocado. Drizzle with remaining sauce.

preparation time 5 minutes **cooking time** 15 minutes **serves** 4
nutritional count per serving 22.6g total fat (8.3g saturated fat); 1768kJ (423 cal); 22.9g carbohydrate; 30.6g protein; 2.9g fibre

Chicken with roasted cherry tomato and basil sauce

500g cherry tomatoes
5 cloves garlic, unpeeled
2 tablespoons olive oil
4 x 200g chicken breast fillets
1/4 cup coarsely chopped fresh basil
1/4 cup (60ml) cream

1 Preheat oven to 200°C/180°C fan-forced.
2 Combine tomatoes, garlic and oil in large shallow baking dish. Roast about 20 minutes or until tomatoes soften. When garlic is cool enough to handle, peel.
3 Meanwhile, cook chicken in heated oiled grill pan until cooked through. Cover; stand 5 minutes.
4 Blend or process garlic and half the tomatoes until smooth; pour into medium saucepan. Add basil and cream; cook, stirring, over low heat, until heated through.
5 Serve chicken topped with sauce and remaining tomatoes.

preparation time 5 minutes **cooking time** 25 minutes **serves** 4
nutritional count per serving 26.8g total fat (9g saturated fat);
1818kJ (435 cal); 3.6g carbohydrate; 44g protein; 2.7g fibre

Grilled chicken with coriander and chilli

8 chicken thigh cutlets (1.6kg)
coriander and chilli paste
2 teaspoons coriander seeds
4 fresh small red thai chillies, chopped coarsely
1 teaspoon ground cumin
2 whole cloves
2 cardamom pods, bruised
¼ teaspoon ground turmeric
10cm stick fresh lemon grass (20g), chopped coarsely
2 medium brown onions (300g), chopped coarsely
4 cloves garlic
⅓ cup (80ml) lime juice
2 teaspoons coarse cooking salt
2 tablespoons peanut oil

1 Make coriander and chilli paste.
2 Pierce chicken all over with sharp knife. Combine paste and chicken in large bowl, rubbing paste into cuts. Cover; refrigerate overnight.
3 Cook chicken, covered, in heated oiled grill pan, 5 minutes. Uncover; cook, turning occasionally, about 20 minutes or until cooked.
4 Serve chicken, if desired, with thin rice noodles and lime wedges.
coriander and chilli paste blend or process ingredients until mixture forms a smooth paste.

preparation time 10 minutes (plus refrigeration time)
cooking time 25 minutes **serves** 4
nutritional count per serving 29.5g total fat (7.8g saturated fat); 2094kJ (501 cal); 5.2g carbohydrate; 53.5g protein; 1.7g fibre

Chicken kofta with red capsicum and walnut sauce

You need to soak 12 bamboo skewers in cold water for at least an hour before use to prevent them from splintering or burning during cooking.

700g chicken mince
1 large brown onion (200g), chopped finely
1½ cups (110g) stale breadcrumbs
1 egg
¼ cup finely chopped fresh coriander
½ teaspoon ground cinnamon
3 teaspoons ground cumin
2 teaspoons ground allspice
6 pitta pockets, halved
100g baby rocket leaves
red capsicum and walnut sauce
2 medium red capsicums (400g)
⅓ cup (35g) roasted walnuts
2 tablespoons stale breadcrumbs
2 tablespoons lemon juice
1 teaspoon sambal oelek
½ teaspoon ground cumin
2 tablespoons olive oil

1 Using hand, combine mince, onion, breadcrumbs, egg, coriander and spices in large bowl; shape ¼-cups of the mixture around each skewer to form slightly flattened sausage shapes. Place kofta on tray, cover; refrigerate 10 minutes.
2 Meanwhile, make red capsicum and walnut sauce.
3 Cook kofta in heated oiled grill pan about 15 minutes or until cooked through. Serve kofta with warmed pitta, rocket and sauce.
red capsicum and walnut sauce quarter capsicums; discard seeds and membranes. Cook in heated oiled grill pan, skin-side down, uncovered, until skin blisters and blackens. Cover capsicum pieces with plastic wrap or paper for 5 minutes; peel away skin. Blend or process capsicum with remaining ingredients until smooth.
preparation time 20 minutes (plus refrigeration time)
cooking time 20 minutes **serves** 4
nutritional count per serving 28.0g total fat (4.7g saturated fat); 3549kJ (849 cal); 87.8g carbohydrate; 57.0g protein; 7.2g fibre

Grilled citrus chicken with orange and pistachio couscous

3 cloves garlic, crushed
1 tablespoon finely chopped fresh oregano
¼ cup (60ml) lemon juice
½ cup (170g) orange marmalade
2 fresh small red thai chillies, chopped finely
4 chicken breast fillets (800g)
2 cups (500ml) chicken stock
2 cups (400g) couscous
2 medium oranges (480g)
2 green onions, sliced thinly
⅓ cup (45g) roasted unsalted pistachios, chopped coarsely

1 Preheat oven to 200°C/180°C fan-forced. Oil and line oven tray.
2 Combine garlic, oregano, juice, marmalade and chilli in medium bowl with chicken.
3 Drain chicken, reserve marmalade mixture; cook chicken in heated oiled grill pan until browned both sides. Place chicken on oven tray, drizzle with reserved marmalade mixture; cook in oven, uncovered, about 10 minutes or until chicken is cooked through.
4 Meanwhile, bring stock to the boil in medium saucepan. Combine couscous with the stock in large heatproof bowl, cover; stand about 5 minutes or until liquid is absorbed, fluffing with fork occasionally. Segment oranges over couscous; stir in onion and nuts.
5 Serve couscous with chicken.

preparation time 10 minutes **cooking time** 15 minutes **serves** 4
nutritional count per serving 18g total fat (4.4g saturated fat); 3620kJ (866 cal); 113g carbohydrate; 60.4g protein; 4.3g fibre

Grilled lamb with paprikash sauce

800g lamb backstraps
1 tablespoon olive oil
1 small brown onion (80g), chopped finely
1 clove garlic, crushed
1 teaspoon smoked paprika
2 teaspoons sweet paprika
pinch cayenne pepper
410g can crushed tomatoes
½ cup (125ml) water

1 Cook lamb in heated oiled grill pan until browned and cooked as desired. Cover; stand 5 minutes then slice thickly.
2 Meanwhile, heat oil in medium saucepan; cook onion, stirring, until onion softens. Add garlic and spices; cook, stirring, about 1 minute or until fragrant. Add undrained tomatoes and the water; bring to the boil. Reduce heat; simmer, uncovered, about 5 minutes or until paprikash sauce thickens slightly.
3 Serve lamb with sauce and, if desired, baked potatoes.

preparation time 5 minutes **cooking time** 10 minutes **serves** 4
nutritional count per serving 12g total fat (3.8g saturated fat);
1241kJ (297 cal); 4.4g carbohydrate; 42.1g protein; 1.6g fibre

Spiced lamb burger with tzatziki

500g lamb mince
½ small red onion (50g), chopped finely
1 egg yolk
½ cup (35g) stale breadcrumbs
2 tablespoons sumac
1 large loaf turkish bread (430g)
250g tzatziki
350g watercress, trimmed
¼ cup (60ml) lemon juice
225g can sliced beetroot, drained

1 Combine mince, onion, egg yolk, breadcrumbs and half the sumac in medium bowl; shape mixture into four patties.
2 Cook patties in heated oiled grill pan until cooked.
3 Meanwhile, preheat grill. Trim ends from bread; cut remaining bread into quarters then halve pieces horizontally. Toast, cut-sides up, under grill.
4 Combine remaining sumac and tzatziki in small bowl. Combine watercress and juice in another bowl.
5 Sandwich patties, tzatziki mixture, beetroot and watercress between bread pieces.

preparation time 20 minutes   **cooking time** 10 minutes   **serves** 4
nutritional count per serving   21.1g total fat (7.5g saturated fat); 2604kJ (623 cal); 60g carbohydrate; 43.8g protein; 8g fibre
tips sumac is a purple-red, astringent spice ground from berries growing on shrubs that flourish wild around the Mediterranean; adds a tart, lemony flavour to dips and dressings and goes well with barbecued meat. Can be found in Middle Eastern food stores.
Ready-made tzatziki is available from supermarkets and delicatessens.

Grilled lamb with spicy peach salsa and spinach salad

800g lamb backstraps
spicy peach salsa
1 small red onion (100g), chopped finely
2 large peaches (440g), chopped finely
2 tablespoons finely chopped fresh flat-leaf parsley
1 fresh long red chilli, chopped finely
1 tablespoon malt vinegar
spinach salad
80g trimmed baby spinach leaves
1 tablespoon malt vinegar
2 teaspoons olive oil
½ teaspoon white sugar
2 tablespoons roasted pine nuts
1 tablespoon dried currants

1 Cook lamb in heated oiled grill pan until cooked as desired. Stand, covered, 10 minutes then slice thinly.
2 Meanwhile, make spicy peach salsa.
3 Make spinach salad.
4 Serve lamb with salsa and salad.
spicy peach salsa combine ingredients in medium bowl.
spinach salad place ingredients in medium bowl; toss gently to combine.

preparation time 20 minutes **cooking time** 10 minutes **serves** 4
nutritional count per serving 25.1g total fat (8.6g saturated fat);
1881kJ (450 cal); 9.8g carbohydrate; 44.6g protein; 2.9g fibre

Moroccan lamb cutlets

1 teaspoon ground coriander
2 teaspoons ground cumin
2 teaspoons sweet paprika
¼ teaspoon cayenne pepper
1 clove garlic, crushed
1 tablespoon finely chopped fresh flat-leaf parsley
2 tablespoons olive oil
24 french-trimmed lamb cutlets (960g)
1 teaspoon cumin seeds, toasted
¼ cup (60g) baba ghanoush

1 Combine ground coriander, ground cumin, sweet paprika, cayenne pepper, garlic, parsley and oil in medium bowl; rub mixture all over lamb.
2 Cook lamb on heated oiled grill pan until cooked as desired.
3 Sprinkle lamb with cumin seeds; serve with baba ghanoush.

preparation time 10 minutes **cooking time** 5 minutes **serves** 6
nutritional count per serving 14.8g total fat (4.7g saturated fat);
974kJ (233 cal); 0.5g carbohydrate; 24.5g protein; 1.1g fibre
tip ready-made baba ghanoush can be purchased from most
supermarkets and delicatessens.

Lemon and garlic lamb cutlets with broad bean, mixed pea and fetta salad

2 tablespoons olive oil
1 tablespoon finely grated lemon rind
2 tablespoons lemon juice
2 cloves garlic, crushed
12 french-trimmed lamb cutlets (600g)
1 ⅓ cups (225g) frozen broad beans
⅔ cup (80g) frozen baby peas
200g snow peas, trimmed, sliced thinly
1 cup coarsely chopped fresh basil
150g fetta cheese, crumbled
1 cup (150g) seeded kalamata olives
lemon dressing
¼ cup (60ml) olive oil
2 tablespoons lemon juice
1 teaspoon dijon mustard

1 Combine oil, rind, juice and garlic in large bowl with lamb.
2 Boil, steam or microwave beans and baby peas, separately, until just tender; drain. Rinse under cold water; drain. Peel away grey-coloured outer shells from broad beans; combine beans and peas in large bowl.
3 Meanwhile, make lemon dressing.
4 Cook lamb, in batches, in heated oiled grill pan until browned both sides and cooked as desired.
5 Place beans and baby peas in large bowl with snow peas, basil, cheese, olives and half of the dressing; toss gently to combine.
6 Serve salad topped with lamb; drizzle with remaining dressing. Sprinkle with a little grated lemon rind, if desired.
lemon dressing place ingredients in screw-top jar; shake well.

preparation time 30 minutes **cooking time** 15 minutes **serves** 4
nutritional count per serving 45.2g total fat (14.9g saturated fat); 2424kJ (580 cal); 17.1g carbohydrate; 27.1g protein; 6.7g fibre

Lamb stack with capsicum, eggplant and pesto

¼ cup (20g) finely grated parmesan cheese
¼ cup (40g) roasted pine nuts
1 clove garlic, quartered
½ cup (125ml) olive oil
1 cup firmly packed fresh basil leaves
1 tablespoon lemon juice
2 medium red capsicums (400g)
1 small eggplant (230g), cut into 8 slices crossways
4 lamb backstraps (800g)

1 To make pesto, blend or process cheese, nuts and garlic with half the oil until combined. Add basil and remaining oil; blend until pesto forms a smooth, thick puree. Stir in juice.
2 Quarter capsicums; discard seeds and membranes. Roast under grill or in very hot oven, skin-side up, until skin blisters and blackens. Cover capsicum pieces with plastic or paper for 5 minutes; peel away skin.
3 Cook eggplant in heated oiled grill pan until tender.
4 Cook lamb, in batches, in same grill pan until cooked as desired. Cover, stand 5 minutes, slice thickly.
5 Make four stacks, on serving plates, starting with eggplant, then lamb and capsicum; spoon pesto over each stack.

preparation time 20 minutes **cooking time** 25 minutes **serves** 4
nutritional count per serving 55.1g total fat (13.5g saturated fat); 2959kJ (708 cal); 5.7g carbohydrate; 47.3g protein; 3.5g fibre

Lamb chops rogan josh with pulao salad

12 lamb loin chops (1.2kg)
½ cup (150g) rogan josh curry paste
1½ cups (300g) basmati rice
¼ teaspoon ground turmeric
1 cardamom pod, bruised
⅓ cup (45g) roasted slivered almonds
⅓ cup (55g) sultanas
⅓ cup firmly packed fresh coriander leaves
⅓ cup coarsely chopped fresh mint
mustard seed dressing
¼ cup (60ml) olive oil
2 tablespoons yellow mustard seeds
¼ cup (60ml) white wine vinegar
1 tablespoon white sugar

1 Combine lamb and paste in large bowl.
2 Make mustard seed dressing.
3 Cook rice, turmeric and cardamom in large saucepan of boiling water until rice is tender; drain.
4 Meanwhile, cook lamb, in batches, in heated oiled grill pan until cooked.
5 Place rice in large bowl with nuts, sultanas, herbs and dressing; toss gently to combine. Serve pulao salad topped with lamb.
mustard seed dressing heat oil in small saucepan; cook seeds, stirring constantly, over low heat, until aromatic and softened. Place seeds, vinegar and sugar in screw-top jar; shake well.

preparation time 10 minutes **cooking time** 20 minutes **serves** 6
nutritional count per serving 41.6g total fat (11.6g saturated fat); 3072kJ (735 cal); 51.7g carbohydrate; 37.2g protein; 4.2g fibre
tip ready-made rogan josh curry paste is available from most supermarkets; adjust the amount according to taste.

Lemon grass lamb with vietnamese vermicelli salad

10cm stick fresh lemon grass (20g), chopped finely
2 tablespoons light soy sauce
1 tablespoon brown sugar
2 tablespoons vegetable oil
3 lamb backstraps (600g)
70g rice vermicelli
2 lebanese cucumbers (260g), seeded, sliced thinly
½ small pineapple (450g), chopped coarsely
1 cup (80g) bean sprouts
1 cup loosely packed fresh coriander leaves
1 cup loosely packed fresh mint leaves
1 large carrot (180g), grated coarsely
1 large butter lettuce, trimmed, leaves separated
chilli lime dressing
¼ cup (60ml) hot water
2 tablespoons fish sauce
1 tablespoon brown sugar
2 tablespoons lime juice
2 fresh small red thai chillies, chopped finely
1 clove garlic, crushed

1 Make chilli lime dressing.
2 Combine lemon grass, sauce, sugar and oil in medium bowl with lamb.
3 Place vermicelli in medium heatproof bowl; cover with boiling water. Stand until just tender; drain. Rinse under cold water; drain.
4 Place vermicelli in large bowl with cucumber, pineapple, sprouts, herbs, carrot and 2 tablespoons of the dressing; toss gently to combine.
5 Cook lamb, both sides, in heated oiled grill pan until cooked. Cover; stand 5 minutes, slice thinly.
6 Top lettuce with salad; serve with lamb, drizzled with remaining dressing.
chilli lime dressing place ingredients in screw-top jar; shake well.

preparation time 25 minutes **cooking time** 20 minutes **serves** 4
nutritional count per serving 22.9g total fat (7.2g saturated fat); 1856kJ (444 cal); 20.6g carbohydrate; 35.9g protein; 6g fibre

Dukkah-crusted lamb cutlets with roasted garlic yogurt

6 cloves garlic, unpeeled
1 teaspoon vegetable oil
1 cup (280g) yogurt
12 french-trimmed lamb cutlets (600g)
dukkah
2 tablespoons roasted hazelnuts
2 tablespoons roasted pistachios
2 tablespoons sesame seeds
2 tablespoons ground coriander
1 tablespoon ground cumin

1 Preheat oven to 180°C/160°C fan-forced.
2 Place garlic on oven tray; drizzle with oil. Roast 10 minutes.
Peel garlic then crush in small bowl with yogurt. Cover; refrigerate.
3 Make dukkah; add lamb, turn to coat in mixture.
4 Cook lamb, both sides, in heated oiled grill pan until cooked.
Serve with roasted garlic yogurt.
dukkah blend or process nuts until chopped finely. Dry-fry seeds and
spices in small frying pan until fragrant; combine with nuts in medium bowl.

preparation time 10 minutes **cooking time** 20 minutes **serves** 4
nutritional count per serving 27.8g total fat (8.7g saturated fat);
1547kJ (370 cal); 5.7g carbohydrate; 22.9g protein; 2.9g fibre
tip dukkah is an Egyptian blend of nuts, spices and seeds, used as a
dip when mixed with oil or into mayonnaise, or sprinkled over meats,
salads or vegetables as a flavour-enhancer. If you don't want to make
this recipe, dukkah is available, ready-made, from delicatessens and
specialty spice shops.

Grilled lamb cutlets with beetroot walnut salad

¼ cup (60ml) sweet chilli sauce
2 tablespoons barbecue sauce
2 teaspoons worcestershire sauce
2 tablespoons white wine vinegar
12 french-trimmed lamb cutlets (600g)
200g fresh green beans
425g can whole baby beetroot, drained, halved
120g firm blue cheese, crumbled
⅓ cup (35g) roasted walnut halves
lemon vinaigrette
1½ tablespoons lemon juice
2 tablespoons olive oil
1 teaspoon caster sugar

1 Make lemon vinaigrette.
2 Combine sauces, vinegar and lamb in large bowl. Stand 5 minutes.
3 Meanwhile, boil, steam or microwave beans until tender; drain. Place beans in medium bowl with beetroot, cheese, nuts and vinaigrette; toss gently to combine.
4 Cook lamb, in batches, in heated oiled grill pan until cooked as desired. Serve lamb with salad.
lemon vinaigrette whisk ingredients in small jug.

preparation time 10 minutes **cooking time** 10 minutes **serves** 4
nutritional count per serving 38.3g total fat (13.9g saturated fat); 2178kJ (521 cal); 17.9g carbohydrate; 24.8g protein; 4.6g fibre

Teriyaki lamb with carrot salad

You need to soak 12 bamboo skewers in cold water for at least an hour before use to prevent them from splintering or burning during cooking.

2 tablespoons japanese soy sauce
2 tablespoons mirin
1 teaspoon caster sugar
600g diced lamb
9 green onions
carrot salad
2 medium carrots (240g), cut into matchsticks
1 cup (80g) bean sprouts
1 small red onion (100g), sliced thinly
1 tablespoon toasted sesame seeds
2 teaspoons japanese soy sauce
1 tablespoon mirin
½ teaspoon caster sugar
2 teaspoons peanut oil

1 Combine sauce, mirin, sugar and lamb in medium bowl.
2 Cut four 3cm-long pieces from trimmed root end of each onion.
3 Thread lamb and onion pieces, alternately, on skewers; cook in heated oiled grill pan, brushing with soy mixture occasionally, until lamb is cooked as desired.
4 Meanwhile, make carrot salad.
5 Serve teriyaki lamb with salad.
carrot salad place ingredients in medium bowl; toss gently to combine.

preparation time 20 minutes **cooking time** 15 minutes **serves** 4
nutritional count per serving 18.4g total fat (6.8g saturated fat);
1467kJ (351 cal); 7.7g carbohydrate; 35g protein; 3.7g fibre

Cantonese beef patties with grilled gai lan

800g beef mince
1 medium brown onion (150g), chopped finely
3 cloves garlic, crushed
2cm piece fresh ginger (10g), grated
1 fresh small red thai chilli, chopped finely
227g can water chestnuts, drained, rinsed, chopped finely
¼ cup finely chopped fresh chives
1 egg
½ cup (35g) fresh breadcrumbs
1 tablespoon hoisin sauce
1 tablespoon water
2 tablespoons oyster sauce
⅓ cup (80ml) hoisin sauce, extra
2 teaspoons sesame oil
1kg gai lan, chopped coarsely

1 Combine mince, onion, two-thirds of the garlic, ginger, chilli, chestnuts, chives, egg, breadcrumbs and hoisin sauce in large bowl; shape mixture into eight patties.
2 Combine the water, oyster sauce, extra hoisin sauce and remaining garlic in small bowl. Reserve ¼ cup (60ml) hoisin mixture.
3 Brush patties with remaining hoisin mixture; cook patties, both sides, in heated oiled grill pan about 10 minutes or until cooked.
4 Heat sesame oil in same grill pan; cook gai lan until wilted. Serve gai lan topped with patties, drizzled with reserved hoisin mixture.

preparation time 30 minutes **cooking time** 15 minutes **serves** 4
nutritional count per serving 20.2g total fat (6.8g saturated fat);
2077kJ (497 cal); 26.6g carbohydrate; 48g protein; 8.3g fibre

Merguez with parmesan polenta triangles

1 litre (4 cups) water
1 cup (170g) polenta
20g butter, chopped
1 cup (80g) finely grated parmesan cheese
8 merguez sausages (640g)
summer salad
1 small red onion (100g), chopped finely
4 green onions, sliced thinly
1 lebanese cucumber (130g), seeded, chopped finely
1 trimmed celery stalk (100g), sliced thinly
1 medium yellow capsicum (200g), chopped finely
½ cup loosely packed fresh flat-leaf parsley leaves
½ cup loosely packed fresh mint leaves
2 teaspoons finely grated lemon rind
2 tablespoons lemon juice
2 tablespoons olive oil
1 tablespoon white wine vinegar

1 Oil deep 19cm-square cake pan.
2 Place the water in large saucepan; bring to the boil. Gradually stir in polenta; simmer, stirring, about 10 minutes or until polenta thickens. Stir in butter and cheese. Spread polenta into pan; cool 10 minutes. Cover; refrigerate 3 hours or until firm.
3 Meanwhile, make summer salad.
4 Turn polenta onto board. Cut polenta into four squares; cut squares into triangles. Cook polenta, both sides, in heated oiled grill pan until browned and hot. Cover to keep warm.
5 Cook sausages in same grill pan until cooked. Serve with polenta triangles and salad.
summer salad place onions, cucumber, celery, capsicum and herbs in large bowl, drizzle with combined rind, juice, oil and vinegar; toss gently to combine.

preparation time 25 minutes (plus refrigeration time)
cooking time 35 minutes **serves** 4
nutritional count per serving 66.8g total fat (25.7g saturated fat); 3975kJ (951 cal); 38.3g carbohydrate; 44g protein; 4.4g fibre

Grilled meatballs and penne

600g beef mince
1 cup (100g) packaged breadcrumbs
¼ cup finely chopped fresh flat-leaf parsley
¼ cup (20g) finely grated parmesan cheese
2 eggs
1 tablespoon olive oil
1 medium white onion (150g), chopped finely
1 clove garlic, crushed
700g bottled tomato pasta sauce
400g can diced tomatoes
½ cup (125ml) chicken stock
¼ cup firmly packed fresh basil leaves
500g penne pasta
2 cups (200g) coarsely grated mozzarella cheese

1 Combine beef, breadcrumbs, parsley, parmesan and eggs in medium bowl. Roll level tablespoons of mixture into balls; flatten slightly.
2 Cook meatballs in heated oiled grill pan until browned all over.
3 Heat oil in deep 3-litre (12-cup) flameproof baking dish. Cook onion and garlic until onion softens. Add sauce, undrained tomatoes, stock and basil; bring to the boil.
4 Add meatballs to sauce; simmer, covered with foil, about 20 minutes or until meatballs are cooked, stirring occasionally.
5 Cook pasta in large saucepan of boiling water until just tender; drain.
6 Preheat grill.
7 Combine pasta with meatballs and sauce, sprinkle with mozzarella; grill until cheese melts and is browned lightly.

preparation time 30 minutes **cooking time** 45 minutes **serves** 6
nutritional count per serving 22.7g total fat (9.7g saturated fat);
3081kJ (737 cal); 82.6g carbohydrate; 46.9g protein; 6.8g fibre

Beef fillet with horseradish mash

4 medium potatoes (800g), chopped coarsely
½ cup (120g) sour cream
¼ cup (60ml) milk
1 tablespoon horseradish cream
600g beef eye fillet
1 cup (250ml) dry red wine
½ cup (125ml) beef stock
1 tablespoon wholegrain mustard

1 Boil, steam or microwave potato until tender; drain. Mash potato with
sour cream and milk in large bowl until smooth; stir in horseradish cream.
2 Meanwhile, slice beef into four equal pieces. Cook in heated oiled grill
pan until browned and cooked as desired. Cover; stand 5 minutes.
3 Combine wine, stock and mustard in medium saucepan; bring to the
boil. Reduce heat; simmer, uncovered, until sauce reduces by half.
4 Serve beef topped with sauce, accompanied by mash and, if desired,
steamed asparagus.

preparation time 15 minutes (plus standing time)
cooking time 30 minutes **serves** 4
nutritional count per serving 22.4g total fat (12.3g saturated fat);
2090kJ (499 cal); 25.0g carbohydrate; 37.7g protein; 2.9g fibre

Mexican-spiced beef with chilli beans

2 cups (400g) dried black beans
2 pasilla chillies (10g)
¼ cup (60ml) boiling water
2 tablespoons olive oil
1 medium brown onion (150g), chopped finely
3 cloves garlic, crushed
¼ cup (70g) tomato paste
4 medium tomatoes (600g), chopped coarsely
½ cup (125ml) water
2 tablespoons lime juice
2 tablespoons brown sugar
1 tablespoon dried marjoram
2 teaspoons smoked paprika
1kg beef rump steak
8 large flour tortillas (320g)
1 small iceberg lettuce, trimmed, shredded
⅔ cup (160g) sour cream
1 small red onion (100g), sliced thinly
⅓ cup firmly packed fresh coriander leaves

1 Place beans in large bowl, cover well with cold water; stand overnight. Rinse under cold water; drain. Cook beans in large saucepan of boiling water, uncovered, until tender; drain. Rinse under cold water; drain.
2 Meanwhile, soak chillies in the boiling water in small bowl 20 minutes; blend or process mixture until smooth.
3 Heat half the oil in large saucepan; cook brown onion and garlic, stirring, until onion softens. Add chilli mixture, paste, tomato, the water, juice and sugar; bring to the boil. Remove from heat; blend or process until smooth.
4 Return chilli mixture to pan with beans; simmer, covered, 20 minutes. Uncover; simmer about 10 minutes or until sauce thickens.
5 Meanwhile, combine marjoram, paprika, remaining oil and beef. Cook in heated oiled grill pan until cooked. Cover beef; stand 10 minutes, slice thinly.
6 Make two foil parcels of four tortillas each; heat parcels both sides in grill pan for 5 minutes or until warm. Serve tortillas with beans, beef, lettuce, sour cream, red onion and coriander.
preparation time 25 minutes (plus standing time)
cooking time 1 hour 20 minutes **serves** 4
nutritional count per serving 49.8g total fat (20.4g saturated fat); 5158kJ (1234 cal); 96.2g carbohydrate; 92g protein; 21.4g fibre

Veal with salsa verde and potato rösti

800g piece veal tenderloin, halved lengthways
4 medium potatoes (800g)
1 egg, beaten lightly
salsa verde
⅔ cup finely chopped fresh flat-leaf parsley
⅓ cup finely chopped fresh mint
⅓ cup finely chopped fresh dill
⅓ cup finely chopped fresh chives
1 tablespoon wholegrain mustard
¼ cup (60ml) lemon juice
¼ cup (50g) drained baby capers, rinsed
2 cloves garlic, crushed
½ cup (125ml) olive oil

1 Make salsa verde.
2 Rub veal with half of the salsa verde; cook in heated oiled grill pan until cooked as desired. Cover veal; stand 5 minutes, slice thickly.
3 Meanwhile, grate potatoes coarsely. Using hands, squeeze excess moisture from potato. Combine potato and egg in medium bowl; divide into eight portions. Cook rösti portions in heated oiled grill pan, flattening with spatula, until browned both sides. Drain on absorbent paper.
4 Serve veal with rösti and remaining salsa verde.
salsa verde combine ingredients in medium bowl.

preparation time 20 minutes **cooking time** 15 minutes **serves** 4
nutritional count per serving 33.2g total fat (5.2g saturated fat);
2537kJ (607 cal); 24.3g carbohydrate; 51.1g protein; 4g fibre

Grilled scotch fillet and chilli jam with white bean and spinach salad

4 x 200g beef scotch fillet steaks
chilli jam
2 medium tomatoes (300g), chopped coarsely
2 tablespoons water
1 tablespoon brown sugar
¼ cup (60ml) sweet chilli sauce
1 fresh long red chilli, chopped finely
2 tablespoons coarsely chopped fresh coriander
white bean and spinach salad
1 clove garlic, crushed
2cm piece fresh ginger (10g), grated
⅓ cup (80ml) lime juice
2 teaspoons sesame oil
¼ cup fresh mint leaves
2 x 420g cans white beans, rinsed, drained
100g baby spinach leaves
1 small red onion (100g), sliced thinly

1 Make chilli jam.
2 Meanwhile, cook beef in heated oiled grill pan until browned both sides and cooked as desired; stand 5 minutes.
3 Meanwhile, make white bean and spinach salad.
4 Serve beef topped with jam, accompanied with salad.
chilli jam bring tomato, the water, sugar, sauce and chilli in medium saucepan to the boil. Reduce heat; simmer, uncovered, about 20 minutes or until jam thickens. Remove from heat; cool 5 minutes. Stir in coriander.
white bean and spinach salad place garlic, ginger, juice and oil in screw-top jar; shake well. Place remaining ingredients in large bowl with dressing; toss gently to combine.

preparation time 20 minutes **cooking time** 35 minutes
serves 4 **makes** I cup chilli jam
nutritional count per serving 14.8g total fat (5.5g saturated fat); 1471kJ (352 cal); 5.5g carbohydrate; 46.7g protein; 4.3g fibre
nutritional count per 1 tablespoon chilli jam 0.2g total fat (0g saturated fat); 59kJ (14 cal); 2.6g carbohydrate; 0.3g protein; 0.6g fibre

163

Spicy beef and bean salad

¼ cup (60ml) olive oil
35g packet taco seasoning mix
600g piece beef eye fillet
2 tablespoons lime juice
1 clove garlic, crushed
420g can four-bean mix, rinsed, drained
310g can corn kernels, rinsed, drained
2 lebanese cucumbers (260g), chopped finely
1 small red onion (100g), chopped finely
1 large red capsicum (350g), chopped finely
½ cup coarsely chopped fresh coriander
1 fresh long red chilli, chopped finely

1 Combine 1 tablespoon of the oil, seasoning and beef in medium bowl.
2 Cook beef in heated grill pan until cooked as desired. Cover; stand
5 minutes, then slice thinly.
3 Meanwhile, whisk remaining oil, juice and garlic in large bowl. Add
remaining ingredients; toss gently to combine.
4 Serve beef with salad; sprinkle with coriander, if desired.

preparation time 10 minutes **cooking time** 20 minutes **serves** 4
nutritional count per serving 22.2g total fat (5.2g saturated fat);
2111kJ (505 cal); 30.9g carbohydrate; 40.4g protein; 9.3g fibre
tip found in most supermarkets, sachets of taco seasoning mix are
meant to duplicate the taste of a Mexican sauce made from cumin,
oregano, chillies and other spices.

Char-grilled steak and vegetables with baba ghanoush

3 cloves garlic, crushed
2 tablespoons olive oil
2 teaspoons finely grated lemon rind
4 x 150g beef eye fillet steaks
2 medium red capsicums (400g), sliced thickly
2 large zucchini (300g), halved crossways, sliced thinly lengthways
½ cup (120g) baba ghanoush
⅓ cup loosely packed fresh mint leaves

1 Combine garlic, oil, rind, steaks, capsicum and zucchini in large bowl.
2 Cook steaks and vegetables, in batches, in heated grill pan until steak is cooked as desired and vegetables are tender.
3 Divide vegetables among serving plates, top with steak. Serve with baba ghanoush and mint.

preparation time 15 minutes **cooking time** 20 minutes **serves** 4
nutritional count per serving 17.3g total fat (4.6g saturated fat);
1354kJ (324 cal); 5.9g carbohydrate; 34.2g protein; 3.6g fibre
tip ready-made baba ghanoush can be purchased from most supermarkets and delicatessens.

Steak sandwich with tarragon and tomato salsa

You need 80g watercress to get the amount of trimmed watercress required for this recipe.

4 x 125g beef scotch fillet steaks
2 cloves garlic, crushed
1 tablespoon dijon mustard
1 tablespoon olive oil
8 thick slices bread (320g)
⅓ cup (100g) mayonnaise
40g trimmed watercress
tarragon and tomato salsa
2 cloves garlic, crushed
3 large egg tomatoes (270g), quartered, sliced thinly
½ small red onion (50g), sliced thinly
1 tablespoon finely chopped fresh tarragon

1 Combine steaks, garlic, mustard and half the oil in medium bowl.
2 Make tarragon and tomato salsa.
3 Cook steaks in heated grill pan until cooked as desired. Remove from heat, cover; stand 5 minutes.
4 Meanwhile, brush both sides of bread with remaining oil; toast in same grill pan. Spread one side of each slice with mayonnaise; sandwich watercress, steak and salsa between slices.
tarragon and tomato salsa combine ingredients in medium bowl.

preparation time 15 minutes **cooking time** 15 minutes **serves** 4
nutritional count per serving 21.6g total fat (4.6g saturated fat);
2161kJ (517 cal); 43.3g carbohydrate; 35g protein; 4.2g fibre
tip you can also use ciabatta, focaccia or even individual turkish bread for this recipe.

Fajitas with salsa cruda and avocado mash

2 tablespoons vegetable oil
⅓ cup (80ml) lime juice
¼ cup coarsely chopped fresh oregano
2 cloves garlic, crushed
¼ cup coarsely chopped fresh coriander
2 teaspoons ground cumin
800g beef skirt steak
1 medium red capsicum (200g), sliced thickly
1 medium green capsicum (200g), sliced thickly
1 medium yellow capsicum (200g), sliced thickly
1 large red onion (300g), sliced thickly
20 small flour tortillas
salsa cruda
2 cloves garlic, crushed
3 medium tomatoes (450g), seeded, chopped finely
1 small white onion (80g), chopped finely
2 trimmed red radishes (30g), chopped finely
1 lebanese cucumber (130g), chopped finely
2 tablespoons coarsely chopped fresh coriander
1 fresh long red chilli, chopped finely
2 tablespoons lime juice
avocado mash
2 small avocados (400g)
2 tablespoons lime juice

1 Combine oil, juice, oregano, garlic, coriander, cumin and beef in large bowl. Cover; refrigerate overnight.
2 Cook beef, capsicums and onion in heated oiled grill pan, in batches, until beef is cooked and vegetables are tender. Remove from pan; cover.
3 Meanwhile, make salsa cruda and avocado mash.
4 Make four foil parcels of five tortillas each; heat parcels both sides in grill pan until tortillas are warm and just softened.
5 Cut beef into 1cm slices; combine with cooked vegetables in large bowl. Serve with salsa cruda, avocado mash and warmed tortillas.
salsa cruda combine ingredients in small bowl.
avocado mash mash avocado and juice in small bowl.
preparation time 25 minutes (plus refrigeration time)
cooking time 15 minutes **serves** 4
nutritional count per serving 46.7g total fat (9.1g saturated fat); 5321kJ (1273 cal); 133.9g carbohydrate; 71.6g protein; 13.2g fibre

Beef teriyaki platter

⅓ cup (80ml) teriyaki sauce
3cm piece fresh ginger (15g), grated
1 clove garlic, crushed
3 x 200g new-york cut steaks, trimmed
500g asparagus, trimmed
8 green onions, trimmed
1 teaspoon wasabi paste
¼ cup (60ml) japanese soy sauce

1 Combine teriyaki sauce, ginger, garlic and beef in large bowl.
Cover; refrigerate 3 hours or overnight.
2 Cook beef in heated oiled grill pan. Remove from heat, cover;
stand 5 minutes.
3 Cook asparagus and onion in heated oiled grill pan until tender.
4 Slice beef thinly; serve with vegetables, accompanied by combined
wasabi and soy sauce.

preparation time 20 minutes (plus refrigeration time)
cooking time 10 minutes **serves** 4
nutritional count per serving 9.3g total fat (3.8g saturated fat);
1032kJ (247 cal); 3.5g carbohydrate; 36.1g protein; 2g fibre

Paprika and cumin-spiced pork cutlets with carrot and olive salad

2 tablespoons olive oil
¼ cup (60ml) lemon juice
2 teaspoons ground cumin
1 tablespoon sweet paprika
4 x 250g pork cutlets
carrot and olive salad
4 medium carrots (480g), halved lengthways, sliced thinly
1 cup (120g) seeded black olives, chopped coarsely
½ cup loosely packed fresh flat-leaf parsley leaves
½ cup loosely packed fresh coriander leaves
2 tablespoons olive oil
2 teaspoons ground cumin
1 tablespoon red wine vinegar
2 teaspoons harissa

1 Combine oil, juice, cumin and paprika in large bowl with cutlets.
2 Cook cutlets in heated oiled grill pan until cooked as desired.
3 Meanwhile, make carrot and olive salad.
4 Serve cutlets with salad.
carrot and olive salad boil, steam or microwave carrot until just tender; drain. Cool 10 minutes. Place carrot in medium bowl with olives, herbs and combined remaining ingredients; toss gently to combine.

preparation time 20 minutes **cooking time** 20 minutes **serves** 4
nutritional count per serving 36.2g total fat (8.6g saturated fat); 2123kJ (508 cal); 13.0g carbohydrate; 31.3g protein; 4.4g fibre
tip harissa is a North African paste made from dried red chillies, garlic, olive oil and caraway seeds; can be used as a rub for meat, an ingredient in sauces and dressings, or eaten as a condiment. It is available from Middle Eastern food shops and some supermarkets.

Mexican pork cutlets with avocado salsa

2 tablespoons taco seasoning mix
2 tablespoons olive oil
4 x 235g pork cutlets
avocado salsa
3 small tomatoes (270g), seeded, chopped finely
1 small avocado (200g), chopped finely
1 lebanese cucumber (130g), seeded, chopped finely
1 tablespoon lime juice
1 tablespoon olive oil

1 Combine seasoning, oil and cutlets in large bowl.
2 Cook cutlets in heated oiled grill pan until browned both sides.
3 Meanwhile, make avocado salsa.
4 Serve cutlets with salsa and, if desired, lime.
avocado salsa combine ingredients in medium bowl.

preparation time 10 minutes **cooking time** 10 minutes **serves** 4
nutritional count per serving 42.2g total fat (10.7g saturated fat);
2241kJ (536 cal); 1.2g carbohydrate; 38g protein; 1.2g fibre
tip found in most supermarkets, sachets of taco seasoning mix are
meant to duplicate the taste of a Mexican sauce made from cumin,
oregano, chillies and other spices.

Grilled pork chops with apple and onion plum sauce

2 medium apples (300g)
1 tablespoon olive oil
1 medium red onion (170g), cut into thin wedges
4 x 280g pork loin chops
½ cup (125ml) plum sauce
¼ cup (60ml) lemon juice
⅓ cup (80ml) chicken stock

1 Cut each unpeeled, uncored apple horizontally into four slices. Heat oil in grill pan; cook apple and onion, turning, until softened.
2 Cook chops in heated oiled grill pan until cooked.
3 Stir sauce, juice and stock into apple mixture; simmer 1 minute.
4 Serve pork chops with sauce.

preparation time 10 minutes **cooking time** 20 minutes **serves** 4
nutritional count per serving 29.7g total fat (9.1g saturated fat);
2404kJ (575 cal); 32g carbohydrate; 45g protein; 1.8g fibre

Jerk pork chops with pumpkin chips

3 long green chillies, chopped coarsely
3 green onions, chopped coarsely
2 cloves garlic, crushed
1 teaspoon ground allspice
1 teaspoon dried thyme
1 teaspoon white sugar
1 tablespoon light soy sauce
1 tablespoon lime juice
4 x 280g pork loin chops
1kg piece pumpkin, trimmed
2 tablespoons vegetable oil
piri piri dipping sauce
⅓ cup (100g) mayonnaise
2 tablespoons piri piri sauce

1 Combine chilli, onion, garlic, allspice, thyme, sugar, sauce, juice and chops in medium bowl.
2 Make piri piri dipping sauce.
3 Cut pumpkin into 7cm chips. Boil, steam or microwave until tender; drain. Combine chips with oil in medium bowl. Cook chips in heated oiled grill pan until browned.
4 Meanwhile, cook chops in grill pan until cooked.
5 Serve chops with chips and dipping sauce.
piri piri dipping sauce combine ingredients in small bowl.

preparation time 15 minutes **cooking time** 25 minutes **serves** 4
nutritional count per serving 39g total fat (9.8g saturated fat);
2554kJ (611 cal); 21.6g carbohydrate; 42.1g protein; 3.6g fibre
tips the use of the word "jerk" in culinary terms refers to a spicy jamaican seasoning used to marinate meat, seafood or poultry before grilling or roasting it. While each cook has his or her particular favourite combination of spices, jerk almost always contains allspice, thyme and chilli.
Piri piri is an Afro-Portuguese hot sauce made from a tiny red chilli of the same name, ground with ginger, garlic, oil and various herbs.

Hoisin pork kebabs

You need to soak 12 bamboo skewers in cold water for at least an hour before use to prevent them from splintering or burning during cooking.

750g pork fillets, sliced
½ cup (125ml) hoisin sauce
2 tablespoons plum sauce
2 cloves garlic, crushed

1 Combine pork, sauces and garlic in medium bowl. Cover; refrigerate 3 hours or overnight.
2 Thread pork onto skewers. Cook in heated oiled grill pan until browned and cooked through.

preparation time 10 minutes (plus refrigeration time)
cooking time 10 minutes **serves** 4
nutritional count per serving 8.2g total fat (2g saturated fat); 1630kJ (390 cal); 33.3g carbohydrate; 42.8g protein; 4.4g fibre

Teriyaki pork with wasabi dressing

750g pork fillets
¼ cup (60ml) teriyaki marinade
50g snow pea sprouts
100g mesclun
50g watercress, trimmed
1 medium red capsicum (200g), sliced thinly
250g yellow teardrop tomatoes, halved
wasabi dressing
1½ teaspoons wasabi powder
¼ cup (60ml) apple cider vinegar
⅓ cup (80ml) vegetable oil
1 tablespoon japanese soy sauce

1 Brush pork with teriyaki marinade. Cook pork, in batches, in heated oiled grill pan, brushing frequently with marinade, until browned and cooked through. Cover to keep warm.
2 Meanwhile, make wasabi dressing.
3 Place sprouts, mesclun, watercress, capsicum and tomato in large bowl with dressing; toss gently to combine.
4 Slice pork; serve with salad.
wasabi dressing blend wasabi with vinegar in small jug; whisk in remaining ingredients.

preparation time 15 minutes **cooking time** 10 minutes **serves** 4
nutritional count per serving 22g total fat (3.4g saturated fat);
1747kJ (418 cal); 7.2g carbohydrate; 46.3g protein; 3.1g fibre

Spiced pork kebabs with honey glaze

You need to soak eight bamboo skewers in cold water for at least an hour before use to prevent them from splintering or burning during cooking.

500g pork fillet
2 cloves garlic, crushed
2 teaspoons cumin seeds
½ teaspoon ground coriander
¼ teaspoon sweet paprika
1 tablespoon olive oil
honey glaze
½ cup (125ml) orange juice
2 tablespoons honey
2 tablespoons barbecue sauce
1 teaspoon dijon mustard

1 Cut pork into 3cm cubes. Combine pork, garlic, cumin, coriander, paprika and oil in medium bowl. Thread pork onto skewers.
2 Cook kebabs in heated oiled grill pan until browned and cooked through.
3 Meanwhile, make honey glaze.
4 Serve kebabs with glaze.
honey glaze stir ingredients in small saucepan over heat until boiling. Reduce heat; simmer 5 minutes or until thickened.

preparation time 15 minutes **cooking time** 15 minutes **makes** 8
nutritional count per kebab 3.3g total fat (0.6g saturated fat);
531kJ (127 cal); 9.7g carbohydrate; 14.3g protein; 0.2g fibre

Pork medallions with gnocchi salad

1 tablespoon olive oil
1 tablespoon balsamic vinegar
1 clove garlic, crushed
800g pork fillets
1 medium red onion (170g), cut into wedges
1 medium red capsicum (200g), quartered
1 medium yellow capsicum (200g), quartered
500g packet potato gnocchi
250g grape tomatoes, halved
1 cup loosely packed fresh basil leaves, torn
1 cup (150g) seeded kalamata olives
balsamic dressing
2 tablespoons olive oil
2 tablespoons balsamic vinegar
1 clove garlic, crushed
1 teaspoon dijon mustard

1 Combine oil, vinegar and garlic in large bowl with pork.
2 Cook onion and capsicums in heated oiled grill pan until tender;
slice capsicums thickly. Transfer onion and capsicums to large bowl;
cover to keep warm.
3 Meanwhile, cook gnocchi in large saucepan of boiling water until
gnocchi float to the surface. Remove from pan with slotted spoon;
place in bowl with grilled vegetables.
4 Cook pork in heated oiled grill pan until cooked as desired. Cover
pork; stand 5 minutes, slice thickly.
5 Make balsamic dressing.
6 Add tomato, basil, olives and dressing to bowl with grilled vegetables
and gnocchi; toss gently to combine. Serve pork with salad.
balsamic dressing place ingredients in screw-top jar; shake well.

preparation time 15 minutes **cooking time** 25 minutes **serves** 4
nutritional count per serving 20.1g total fat (4.1g saturated fat);
2546kJ (609 cal); 51.1g carbohydrate; 51.9g protein; 6.4g fibre

Pork, kumara mash and apple salsa

2 large kumara (1kg), chopped coarsely
20g butter
2 tablespoons finely chopped fresh sage
4 x 200g pork butterfly steaks
1 tablespoon olive oil
2 cloves garlic, crushed
apple salsa
1 large green apple (200g), chopped finely
1 small red onion (100g), chopped finely
1 clove garlic, crushed
1 tablespoon finely chopped fresh sage
1 tablespoon olive oil

1 Make apple salsa.
2 Boil, steam or microwave kumara until tender; drain. Mash kumara with butter in large bowl until smooth; stir in half the sage.
3 Meanwhile, combine steaks, oil, garlic and remaining sage in large bowl.
4 Cook steaks in heated oiled grill pan until browned.
5 Serve pork with mash and salsa.
apple salsa combine ingredients in small bowl.

preparation time 10 minutes **cooking time** 20 minutes **serves** 4
nutritional count per serving 34.1g total fat (10.8g saturated fat);
3327kJ (796 cal); 65.8g carbohydrate; 51.5g protein; 9.1g fibre

Grilled zucchini with pumpkin and couscous

½ cup (100g) couscous
½ cup (125ml) boiling water
2 tablespoons lemon juice
2 teaspoons olive oil
¼ cup (40g) pine nuts
1 clove garlic, crushed
½ small red onion (50g), chopped finely
1 teaspoon sweet smoked paprika
½ teaspoon ground cumin
½ teaspoon cayenne pepper
½ small red capsicum (75g), chopped finely
200g piece pumpkin, chopped finely
2 tablespoons finely chopped fresh flat-leaf parsley
6 medium zucchini (720g), halved lengthways
preserved lemon yogurt
½ cup (140g) greek-style yogurt
2 tablespoons finely chopped preserved lemon
2 tablespoons water

1 Make preserved lemon yogurt.
2 Combine couscous with the water and juice in large heatproof bowl, cover; stand about 5 minutes or until water is absorbed, fluffing with fork occasionally.
3 Heat oil in large saucepan; cook nuts, stirring, until browned. Add garlic, onion and spices; cook, stirring, until onion softens. Add capsicum and pumpkin; cook, stirring, until pumpkin is tender. Stir in couscous and parsley.
4 Meanwhile, cook zucchini in heated oiled grill pan until just tender.
5 Serve zucchini topped with couscous and drizzled with yogurt.
preserved lemon yogurt combine ingredients in small bowl.

preparation time 20 minutes **cooking time** 20 minutes **serves** 4
nutritional count per serving 12.7g total fat (2.5g saturated fat);
1200kJ (287 cal); 30.1g carbohydrate; 10.1g protein; 4.9g fibre
tip preserved lemons, whole or quartered salted lemons preserved in olive oil and lemon juice, are a North African specialty. Available from delicatessens and specialty food shops. Use the rind only and rinse well under cold water before using.

Radicchio, pumpkin and haloumi salad

1kg piece pumpkin, cut into 12 wedges
180g haloumi cheese
¼ cup (60ml) lemon juice
2 tablespoons olive oil
1 tablespoon drained baby capers, rinsed
1 medium radicchio (200g), trimmed, leaves separated
½ cup firmly packed fresh flat-leaf parsley leaves
¼ cup (50g) roasted pepitas

1 Boil, steam or microwave pumpkin until tender; drain.
2 Cut cheese horizontally into four slices, cut each slice into four triangles.
3 Cook pumpkin and cheese, in batches, in heated oiled grill pan
until browned.
4 Meanwhile, place juice, oil and capers in screw-top jar; shake well.
5 Place radicchio in large bowl with dressing and parsley; toss gently to
combine. Divide salad among serving plates; top with pumpkin, cheese
and pepitas.

preparation time 10 minutes **cooking time** 20 minutes **serves** 4
nutritional count per serving 22g total fat (6.8g saturated fat);
1363kJ (326 cal); 15.2g carbohydrate; 14.8g protein; 5.2g fibre

Asparagus with balsamic dressing

400g asparagus, trimmed
⅓ cup (80ml) extra virgin olive oil
½ tablespoons balsamic vinegar
2 medium tomatoes (380g), peeled, seeded, chopped finely
2 tablespoons small fresh basil leaves

1 Cook asparagus in heated oiled grill pan until browned and tender.
2 Serve asparagus drizzled with combined oil, vinegar and tomato; sprinkle with basil.

preparation time 10 minutes **cooking time** 5 minutes **serves** 4
nutritional count per serving 18.4g total fat (2.6g saturated fat); 790kJ (189 cal); 2.8g carbohydrate; 2.7g protein; 2.2g fibre

Grilled vegetables with garlic rosemary dressing

1 medium red capsicum (200g)
1 medium yellow capsicum (200g)
¼ cup (60ml) olive oil
1 clove garlic, crushed
1 teaspoon finely grated lemon rind
2 teaspoons finely chopped fresh rosemary
1 medium red onion (170g), cut into wedges
2 small leeks (400g), trimmed, cut into 2cm pieces
1 medium eggplant (300g), sliced thickly
2 medium zucchini (240g), sliced thickly
4 flat mushrooms (320g), quartered
3 cloves garlic, unpeeled
⅓ cup (100g) mayonnaise
1 tablespoon lemon juice

1 Quarter capsicums, discard seeds and membranes. Roast under grill or in very hot oven, skin-side up, until skin blisters and blackens. Cover capsicum pieces in plastic or paper 5 minutes; peel away skin, slice thickly.
2 Combine oil, crushed garlic, rind and half the rosemary in small bowl.
3 Brush onion, leek, eggplant, zucchini, mushrooms and unpeeled garlic with oil mixture; cook vegetables, in batches, in heated oiled grill pan until tender.
4 Squeeze cooked garlic into small jug; discard skins. Whisk in remaining rosemary, mayonnaise and juice. Serve vegetables with dressing.

preparation time 30 minutes **cooking time** 30 minutes **serves** 4
nutritional count per serving 22.8g total fat (2.9g saturated fat);
1325kJ (317 cal); 16.9g carbohydrate; 7.9g protein; 8.4g fibre

Tofu and vegie burger

300g firm silken tofu
1 tablespoon olive oil
1 medium brown onion (150g), chopped finely
2 cloves garlic, crushed
¼ teaspoon sweet paprika
1 teaspoon ground turmeric
2 teaspoons ground coriander
1 small zucchini (90g), grated coarsely
2 cups (140g) fresh breadcrumbs
¾ cup (190g) hummus
¼ cup (70g) greek-style yogurt
1 loaf turkish bread (430g)
⅓ cup coarsely chopped fresh mint
½ cup coarsely chopped fresh flat-leaf parsley
1 green onion, sliced thinly
30g snow pea sprouts, trimmed

1 Pat tofu dry with absorbent paper. Spread tofu, in single layer, on absorbent-paper-lined tray; cover with more paper, stand 20 minutes.
2 Meanwhile, heat oil in medium frying pan; cook brown onion and garlic, stirring, until onion softens. Add spices; cook, stirring, until fragrant.
3 Combine onion mixture in large bowl with tofu, zucchini and breadcrumbs; shape into four patties. Cover; refrigerate 30 minutes.
4 Meanwhile, combine hummus and yogurt in small bowl.
5 Cut bread into four pieces. Split each piece in half horizontally; toast cut sides in heated oiled grill pan.
6 Cook patties in same oiled grill pan until browned both sides and hot.
7 Spread bread with hummus mixture; sandwich combined mint, parsley and green onion, patties and sprouts between bread pieces.

preparation time 20 minutes (plus standing time)
cooking time 20 minutes (plus refrigeration time) **serves** 4
nutritional count per serving 24.1g total fat (4.6g saturated fat); 2880kJ (689 cal); 81.5g carbohydrate; 30.2g protein; 11.7g fibre

Paprika and parmesan polenta with walnut and capsicum salsa

20g butter
2 medium brown onions (300g), sliced thinly
1 tablespoon brown sugar
1 litre (4 cups) water
1⅓ cups (225g) polenta
2 teaspoons smoked paprika
1 tablespoon red wine vinegar
1 cup (80g) coarsely grated parmesan cheese
walnut and capsicum salsa
2 large red capsicums (700g)
1½ cups (150g) roasted walnuts, chopped coarsely
1 tablespoon red wine vinegar
¼ cup (60ml) walnut oil
1 clove garlic, crushed
½ cup coarsely chopped fresh flat-leaf parsley

1 Melt butter in medium frying pan; cook onion, stirring, 5 minutes or until softened. Add sugar and 2 tablespoons of the water; cook 2 minutes or until onion caramelises. Cover to keep warm.
2 Oil deep 22cm-round cake pan. Bring remaining water to the boil in medium saucepan. Gradually add polenta and paprika, stirring constantly. Simmer, stirring, about 8 minutes or until polenta thickens. Stir in vinegar and cheese then spread half the polenta into pan. Spread onion mixture over polenta, spread remaining polenta over onion. Cover; refrigerate 3 hours or until firm.
3 Meanwhile, make walnut and capsicum salsa.
4 Turn polenta onto board; cut into six wedges. Cook polenta, both sides, in heated oiled grill pan until browned and hot. Serve with salsa.
walnut and capsicum salsa quarter capsicums, discard seeds and membranes. Roast under grill or in very hot oven, skin-side up, until skin blisters and blackens. Cover capsicum pieces in plastic or paper for 5 minutes; peel away skin, chop coarsely. Combine capsicum in small bowl with remaining ingredients.
preparation time 20 minutes
cooking time 45 minutes (plus refrigeration time) **serves** 6
nutritional count per serving 51.8g total fat (10.6g saturated fat); 3210kJ (768 cal); 51.9g carbohydrate; 21.2g protein; 7.1g fibre

Grilled asian vegetables

400g baby buk choy, trimmed, halved lengthways
2 tablespoons peanut oil
175g broccolini, halved
100g snow peas, trimmed
200g baby corn, halved lengthways
2 tablespoons mirin
1 tablespoon vegetarian mushroom oyster sauce
1 tablespoon light soy sauce
1 clove garlic, crushed
1 teaspoon white sugar
½ teaspoon sesame oil

1 Boil, steam or microwave buk choy until wilted; drain. Brush with half the peanut oil; cook in heated oiled flat pan until tender.
2 Combine broccolini, peas and corn in large bowl with remaining peanut oil; mix well. Cook vegetables, in batches, in same grill pan until tender.
3 Combine mirin, sauces, garlic, sugar and sesame oil in large bowl; add grilled vegetables, mix well.

preparation time 10 minutes **cooking time** 10 minutes **serves** 4
nutritional count per serving 10.7g total fat (1.8g saturated fat);
811kJ (194 cal); 13.4g carbohydrate; 6.5g protein; 6.1g fibre
tip "vegetarian" mushroom oyster sauce is made from blended mushrooms and soy, and is available from health food stores and some supermarkets.

Grilled asparagus with tomato

You need four bunches of asparagus for this recipe.

¼ cup (60ml) olive oil
¼ cup (60ml) white wine vinegar
2 teaspoons fresh lemon thyme leaves
2 cloves garlic, crushed
2 large red onions (600g), cut into wedges
680g asparagus, trimmed, halved
250g cherry tomatoes, halved

1 Combine oil, vinegar, thyme, garlic and onion in large bowl. Drain onion; reserve vinegar mixture in bowl.
2 Cook onion in heated oiled grill pan until soft and browned lightly.
3 Meanwhile, cook asparagus and tomato, in batches, in same oiled grill pan until tender.
4 Combine vegetables in bowl with reserved vinegar mixture.

preparation time 10 minutes **cooking time** 20 minutes **serves** 4
nutritional count per serving 14.1g total fat (1.9g saturated fat); 895kJ (214 cal); 12g carbohydrate; 6.8g protein; 5.8g fibre

Marinated mixed mushrooms

2 cloves garlic, crushed
4cm piece fresh ginger (20g), grated
⅓ cup (80ml) light soy sauce
2 tablespoons mirin
2 tablespoons sake
2 tablespoons peanut oil
1 tablespoon white sugar
200g oyster mushrooms
200g shiitake mushrooms
200g button mushrooms
200g swiss brown mushrooms
200g enoki mushrooms
4 green onions, sliced diagonally

1 Combine garlic, ginger, sauce, mirin, sake, oil, sugar and mushrooms in large bowl. Cover; refrigerate 2 hours.
2 Drain mushrooms; reserve marinade in bowl. Cook mushrooms, in batches, in heated oiled grill pan until tender.
3 Combine mushrooms and onion in bowl with reserved marinade.

preparation time 15 minutes (plus refrigeration time)
cooking time 10 minutes **serves** 4
nutritional count per serving 9.8g total fat (1.7g saturated fat);
890kJ (213 cal); 14.9g carbohydrate; 9.2g protein; 7.7g fibre

Tabbouleh with grilled eggplant

3 small tomatoes (270g)
¼ cup (40g) burghul
2 large eggplants (1kg)
2 tablespoons olive oil
2 teaspoons sumac
4 cups coarsely chopped fresh flat-leaf parsley
1 cup coarsely chopped fresh mint
1 medium red onion (170g), chopped finely
2 tablespoons lemon juice
2 tablespoons olive oil, extra

1 Chop tomatoes finely, retaining as much juice as possible. Place tomato and tomato juice on top of burghul in small bowl. Cover; refrigerate about 2 hours or until burghul softens.
2 Cut each eggplant into 8 wedges. Brush wedges with combined oil and sumac; cook in heated grill pan until tender.
3 Meanwhile, combine burghul mixture with herbs, onion, juice and extra oil.
4 Serve tabbouleh with eggplant, and yogurt, if desired.

preparation time 15 minutes (plus refrigeration time)
cooking time 10 minutes **serves** 4
nutritional count per serving 19.5g total fat (2.6g saturated fat); 1225kJ (293 cal); 17.1g carbohydrate; 6.7g protein; 12.6g fibre
tip sumac is a purple-red, astringent spice ground from berries growing on shrubs that flourish wild around the Mediterranean; adds a tart, lemony flavour to dips and dressings and goes well with barbecued meat. Can be found in Middle Eastern food stores.

Char-grilled radicchio parcels

3 cloves garlic, crushed
1 cup (150g) drained semi-dried tomatoes, chopped coarsely
420g bocconcini cheese
1 cup coarsely chopped fresh basil
2 x 420g cans white beans, rinsed, drained
24 large radicchio leaves
1 tablespoon balsamic vinegar

1 Combine garlic, tomato, cheese, basil and beans in large bowl.
2 Plunge radicchio into large saucepan of boiling water then drain immediately; submerge in iced water to halt cooking process. When cool, drain; pat dry with absorbent paper.
3 Slightly overlap 2 leaves; centre about a quarter cup of bean mixture on leaves then roll, folding in edges to enclose filling. Repeat with remaining bean mixture and leaves.
4 Cook parcels, seam-side down, in heated oiled grill pan until filling is hot. Serve parcels drizzled with vinegar.

preparation time 20 minutes **cooking time** 5 minutes **serves** 4
nutritional count per serving 20g total fat (11g saturated fat);
1659kJ (397 cal); 18.9g carbohydrate; 28.7g protein; 13.8g fibre

the
barbecue

Seafood antipasto

12 uncooked large king prawns (840g)
8 sardine fillets (360g), butterflied
8 whole cleaned baby octopus (720g)
2 cloves garlic, crushed
2 tablespoons olive oil
1 loaf ciabatta (440g), sliced thickly
170g asparagus, halved lengthways
200g grape tomatoes
1 cup (150g) seeded kalamata olives
250g haloumi cheese, sliced lengthways into 8 pieces
garlic chilli dressing
4 cloves garlic, crushed
1 tablespoon finely grated lime rind
¼ cup (60ml) lime juice
2 fresh small red thai chillies, chopped finely

1 Shell and devein prawns, leaving heads and tails intact. Combine prawns in large bowl with sardines, octopus, half the garlic and half the oil. Cover; refrigerate 3 hours or overnight.
2 Combine remaining garlic and oil in small bowl; brush bread slices, both sides, with garlic oil. Toast bread, both sides, on heated oiled flat plate.
3 Cook asparagus, tomatoes, olives and cheese, in batches, on flat plate, until asparagus is tender.
4 Meanwhile, make garlic chilli dressing.
5 Cook seafood, in batches, on flat plate until cooked as desired; drizzle with dressing. Serve with vegetables and cheese.
garlic chilli dressing place ingredients in screw-top jar; shake well.

preparation time 25 minutes (plus refrigeration time)
cooking time 20 minutes **serves** 4
nutritional count per serving 51.1g total fat (15.4g saturated fat); 4840kJ (1158 cal); 63.2g carbohydrate; 108g protein; 6.2g fibre
tip the seafood can be prepared the night before, as can the dressing.

Thai fish burger

500g white fish fillets, chopped coarsely
1 tablespoon fish sauce
1 tablespoon kecap manis
1 clove garlic, quartered
1 fresh small red thai chilli, chopped coarsely
50g green beans, trimmed, chopped coarsely
¼ cup (20g) fried shallots
¼ cup coarsely chopped fresh coriander
60g baby spinach leaves
1 lebanese cucumber (130g), seeded, sliced thinly
1 tablespoon lime juice
2 teaspoons brown sugar
2 teaspoons fish sauce, extra
4 hamburger buns (360g)
⅓ cup (80ml) sweet chilli sauce

1 Blend or process fish, sauce, kecap manis, garlic and chilli until smooth; transfer mixture to large bowl. Add beans, shallots and coriander; mix well. Shape mixture into four patties.
2 Cook patties on heated oiled flat plate about 15 minutes or until cooked.
3 Combine spinach, cucumber, juice, sugar and extra sauce in medium bowl.
4 Split buns in half; toast cut-sides. Sandwich salad, patties and sweet chilli sauce between bun halves.

preparation time 20 minutes **cooking time** 15 minutes **serves** 4
nutritional count per serving 5.3g total fat (0.7g saturated fat);
1722kJ (412 cal); 55.2g carbohydrate; 32g protein; 5.7g fibre
tip we used blue-eye in this recipe, but you can use any firm white fish.

Prawn and chorizo skewers with bean and tomato salad

24 uncooked medium king prawns (1kg)
4 cloves garlic, crushed
2 tablespoons olive oil
150g green beans, trimmed, halved
3 medium egg tomatoes (225g), quartered
2 tablespoons roasted pine nuts
¼ cup coarsely chopped fresh flat-leaf parsley
8 x 20cm stalks fresh rosemary
2 chorizo sausages (340g), sliced thickly
lime mustard dressing
2 tablespoons olive oil
2 tablespoons lime juice
1 tablespoon wholegrain mustard
2 cloves garlic, crushed

1 Shell and devein prawns, leaving tails intact. Combine prawns in medium bowl with garlic and oil. Cover; refrigerate 3 hours or overnight.
2 Make lime mustard dressing.
3 Boil, steam or microwave beans until just tender; drain. Rinse under cold water; drain. Place beans in medium bowl with tomato, nuts, parsley and dressing; toss gently to combine.
4 Drain prawns, discard marinade. Remove leaves from bottom two-thirds of each rosemary stalk; thread prawns and chorizo, alternately, onto rosemary skewers. Cook skewers on heated oiled grill plate until prawns are changed in colour and chorizo is browned.
lime mustard dressing place ingredients in screw-top jar; shake well.

preparation time 25 minutes (plus refrigeration time)
cooking time 10 minutes **serves** 4
nutritional count per serving 49.9g total fat (12.3g saturated fat); 2730kJ (653 cal); 5.4g carbohydrate; 45g protein; 3.4g fibre

Cajun seafood kebabs with avocado salsa

You need to soak 12 bamboo skewers in cold water for at least an hour before use to prevent them from splintering or burning during cooking.

36 uncooked medium prawns (1.6kg)
800g white boneless fish fillets
2 tablespoons cajun seasoning
2 teaspoons ground cumin
2 tablespoons finely chopped fresh oregano
2 cloves garlic, crushed
¼ cup (60ml) olive oil
avocado salsa
3 medium tomatoes (450g), seeded, chopped finely
1 small red onion (100g), chopped finely
1 large avocado (320g), chopped finely
2 tablespoons finely chopped fresh coriander
2 tablespoons lemon juice
1 tablespoon olive oil
½ teaspoon white sugar

1 Shell and devein prawns, leaving tails intact. Cut fish into 3cm cubes.
2 Combine prawns and fish in large bowl with remaining ingredients. Cover; refrigerate at least 20 minutes or until required.
3 Meanwhile, make avocado salsa.
4 Thread prawns and fish onto skewers; cook on heated oiled grill plate until just cooked. Serve kebabs with salsa.
avocado salsa combine ingredients in medium bowl.

preparation time 40 minutes (plus refrigeration time)
cooking time 10 minutes   **serves** 6
nutritional count per serving 25.6g total fat (4.9g saturated fat); 1952kJ (467 cal); 2.3g carbohydrate; 56g protein; 1.4g fibre
tip cajun seasoning is used to give an authentic USA Deep South spicy cajun flavour to food, this packaged blend of assorted herbs and spices can include paprika, basil, onion, fennel, thyme, cayenne and tarragon.

Balmain bugs with garlic herbed butter

8 uncooked balmain bugs (1.6kg)
4 large flat mushrooms (360g)
100g curly endive, chopped coarsely
herb butter
125g butter, softened
2 teaspoons finely grated lemon rind
2 tablespoons lemon juice
2 tablespoons finely chopped fresh chives
2 tablespoons coarsely chopped fresh flat-leaf parsley
2 tablespoons coarsely chopped fresh tarragon
1 clove garlic, crushed

1 Place bugs upside down on board; cut tail from body, discard body.
Using scissors, cut soft shell from underneath tails to expose meat;
cut tails in half lengthways. Discard back vein.
2 Make herbed butter.
3 Melt half the herb butter in small saucepan. Brush mushrooms with
half the melted butter; cook on heated oiled grill plate until tender.
4 Brush bugs with remaining melted butter mixture; cook on grill plate.
5 Serve endive and mushrooms with bug halves; top with remaining
herb butter.
herb butter beat butter, rind and juice in small bowl with electric mixer
until light and fluffy; stir in herbs and garlic.

preparation time 30 minutes **cooking time** 20 minutes **serves** 4
nutritional count per serving 27.1g total fat (17.1g saturated fat);
1584kJ (379 cal); 2.1g carbohydrate; 30.4g protein; 3.2g fibre
tip we used balmain bugs in this recipe, but you could also use
uncooked moreton bay bugs or fresh scampi.

Kaffir lime and lemon grass grilled trout

10cm stick fresh lemon grass (20g), chopped coarsely
4cm piece fresh ginger (20g), sliced thickly
2 cloves garlic, quartered
2 tablespoons peanut oil
1 tablespoon sweet chilli sauce
1 tablespoon lime juice
2 green onions, chopped finely
1 whole ocean trout (2.4kg)
1 lime, peeled, sliced thinly
10cm stick fresh lemon grass (20g), sliced diagonally
1 kaffir lime leaf, shredded thinly
⅓ cup loosely packed fresh coriander leaves
1 lime, cut into wedges

1 Blend or process chopped lemon grass, ginger, garlic, oil, sauce and juice until smooth; stir in onion.
2 Place long piece of baking paper on bench; place fish on paper. Fill cavity with lemon grass mixture.
3 Score fish three times both sides through thickest part of flesh; seal cuts with lime slices; sprinkle fish with sliced lemon grass and lime leaf. Fold paper over fish to completely enclose, then wrap fish tightly in foil.
4 Cook fish on heated oiled grill plate 25 minutes; turn, cook for further 20 minutes or until cooked through.
5 Serve fish sprinkled with coriander; serve with lime wedges.

preparation time 20 minutes **cooking time** 45 minutes **serves** 6
nutritional count per serving 14.3g total fat (3g saturated fat); 1262kJ (302 cal); 1.2g carbohydrate; 41.4g protein; 0.7g fibre

Barbecued squid skewers with chilli dipping sauce

You need to soak 48 bamboo skewers in cold water for at least an hour before use to prevent them from splintering or burning during cooking.

8 cleaned baby squid hoods (500g)
2 tablespoons sweet chilli sauce
2 teaspoons finely grated lime rind
2 tablespoons peanut oil
chilli dipping sauce
2 tablespoons sweet chilli sauce
2 tablespoons lime juice
1 tablespoon fish sauce
1 fresh small red thai chilli, chopped finely
1 tablespoon finely chopped fresh coriander

1 Make chilli dipping sauce.
2 Cut squid hoods down centre to open out; score inside in diagonal pattern. Halve hoods lengthways; cut each piece into three strips. Thread one strip onto each skewer; place, in single layer, in large shallow dish.
3 Combine sauce, rind and oil in small bowl; pour over squid. Cook squid on heated oiled grill plate.
4 Serve skewers with dipping sauce and, if desired, coriander leaves.
chilli dipping sauce place ingredients in screw-top jar; shake well.

preparation time 25 minutes **cooking time** 5 minutes **makes** 48
nutritional count per skewer 3.7g total fat (0.8g saturated fat); 288kJ (69 cal); 1.5g carbohydrate; 7.2g protein; 0.4g fibre

Barbecued prawns with chilli lime dressing

1.7kg uncooked large king prawns
¼ cup coarsely chopped fresh coriander
chilli lime dressing
⅓ cup (80ml) lime juice
⅓ cup (80ml) lemon juice
½ cup (125ml) olive oil
2 cloves garlic, crushed
2 teaspoons caster sugar
2 teaspoons sea salt flakes
3 fresh long red chillies, sliced thinly

1 Make chilli lime dressing.
2 Using small sharp knife, devein prawns, leaving heads and shells intact. Combine prawns in large bowl with half the dressing.
3 Cook prawns on heated oiled grill plate.
4 Stir coriander into remaining dressing; serve with prawns.
chilli lime dressing combine ingredients in small bowl.

preparation time 30 minutes   **cooking time** 5 minutes   **serves** 4
nutritional count per serving 29.8g total fat (4.2g saturated fat);
1914kJ (458 cal); 3.4g carbohydrate; 44.1g protein; 0.4g fibre

Raspberry vinaigrette octopus

1kg baby octopus
2 cloves garlic, crushed
⅓ cup (80ml) raspberry vinegar
⅓ cup (80ml) olive oil
¼ cup finely chopped fresh oregano

1 Remove and discard heads and beaks from octopus.
2 Combine octopus in large bowl with remaining ingredients. Cover; refrigerate at least 20 minutes or until required.
3 Drain octopus over small bowl; reserve marinade. Cook octopus on heated oiled grill plate, brushing occasionally with reserved marinade, until browned and tender.

preparation time 15 minutes (plus refrigeration time)
cooking time 10 minutes **serves** 4
nutritional count per serving 20.9g total fat (3.2g saturated fat); 1438kJ (344 cal); 1.6g carbohydrate; 36.9g protein; 0.3g fibre

Lime and coriander octopus

1.25kg baby octopus
2 tablespoons sweet chilli sauce
1 tablespoon kecap manis
¼ cup (60ml) lime juice
2 cloves garlic, crushed
2 tablespoons finely chopped fresh coriander
2 medium limes, sliced thickly

1 Remove and discard heads and beaks from octopus; cut each octopus in half.
2 Combine octopus with sauce, kecap manis, juice, garlic and coriander in large bowl. Cover; refrigerate at least 20 minutes or until required.
3 Drain octopus; discard marinade. Cook octopus and lime slices on heated oiled grill plate until octopus is just cooked and lime slices are browned both sides.

preparation time 20 minutes (plus refrigeration time)
cooking time 20 minutes **serves** 4
nutritional count per serving 3.7g total fat (0.8g saturated fat); 1053kJ (252 cal); 4.7g carbohydrate; 47g protein; 1.6g fibre

Spiced whole fish with nutty rice

You need to cook about ⅔ cup (130g) rice for this recipe.

2 tablespoons ground coriander
1 tablespoon ground cumin
2 teaspoons mustard powder
2 teaspoons sweet paprika
⅓ cup (80ml) peanut oil
2kg whole white fish
seasoning
60g butter
1 medium brown onion (150g), chopped finely
2 cloves garlic, crushed
2 teaspoons mild curry powder
2 cups cooked medium-grain white rice
½ cup (70g) coarsely chopped pistachios, roasted
2 tablespoons finely chopped fresh flat-leaf parsley
2 tablespoons finely chopped fresh coriander
2 teaspoons finely grated lemon rind

1 Dry-fry spices in small frying pan, stirring, until fragrant, cool; stir in oil.
2 Make seasoning.
3 Cut fish three times on each side. Place fish on large sheet of oiled foil. Fill fish cavity with seasoning; brush fish all over with spice mixture. Seal foil to enclose fish.
4 Cook fish on heated oiled grill plate, turning occasionally, until fish is cooked through.
seasoning heat butter in small saucepan; cook onion, garlic and curry powder, stirring, until onion is soft. Combine onion mixture with remaining ingredients in medium bowl.

preparation time 15 minutes **cooking time** 25 minutes **serves** 6
nutritional count per serving 29.2g total fat (9.2g saturated fat); 1927kJ (461 cal); 19.1g carbohydrate; 30g protein; 2g fibre
tip we used snapper in this recipe, but you can use any firm white fish.

Cumin fish cutlets
with coriander chilli sauce

6 x 250g white fish cutlets
2 teaspoons cumin seeds
coriander chilli sauce
8 green onions, chopped coarsely
3 cloves garlic, quartered
2 fresh small red thai chillies, chopped coarsely
1 tablespoon coarsely chopped coriander root
2 tablespoons brown sugar
2 tablespoons fish sauce
¼ cup (60ml) lime juice

1 Make coriander chilli sauce.
2 Sprinkle one side of each fish cutlet with seeds; cook cutlets on heated oiled grill plate until just cooked.
3 Serve cutlets with sauce.
coriander chilli sauce blend or process onion, garlic, chilli, coriander and sugar until finely chopped. Add sauce and juice; blend until combined.

preparation time 10 minutes **cooking time** 10 minutes **serves** 6
nutritional count per serving 4.5g total fat (1.4g saturated fat); 974kJ (233 cal); 5.5g carbohydrate; 41.8g protein; 0.7g fibre

Cajun fish fillets with tomato salsa

1 teaspoon chilli powder
1 tablespoon garlic salt
2 tablespoons dried oregano
2 tablespoons dried thyme
2 teaspoons sweet paprika
4 x 240g white fish fillets
30g butter, melted
1 clove garlic, crushed
1 tablespoon olive oil
4 corn tortillas
tomato salsa
4 medium tomatoes (600g), seeded, chopped finely
1 small red onion (100g), chopped finely
1 tablespoon olive oil
1 tablespoon finely chopped fresh oregano

1 Make tomato salsa.
2 Combine chilli, garlic salt, oregano, thyme and paprika in small bowl.
Brush fish all over with butter; coat with spice mixture.
3 Cook fish on heated oiled grill pan until just cooked. Cover to keep warm.
4 Meanwhile, preheat oven to 220°C/200°C fan-forced.
5 Place crushed garlic in small bowl with oil; brush oil mixture over
both sides of tortillas. Place on oven tray; bake 5 minutes or until crisp.
Cut each tortilla into eight pieces.
6 Serve fish with tortilla triangles and salsa.
tomato salsa combine ingredients in medium bowl.

preparation time 25 minutes **cooking time** 15 minutes **serves** 4
nutritional count per serving 22g total fat (7.2g saturated fat);
2132kJ (510 cal); 21.6g carbohydrate; 54.7g protein; 3.6g fibre
tip we used orange roughy in this recipe, but you can use any firm
white fish.

Fish cutlets with salsa

4 x 250g white fish cutlets
salsa
2 lebanese cucumbers (260g), seeded, chopped finely
2 medium radishes (70g), chopped finely
4 medium egg tomatoes (300g), seeded, chopped finely
1 medium yellow capsicum (200g), seeded, chopped finely
½ teaspoon Tabasco sauce
1 tablespoon sherry vinegar

1 Make salsa.
2 Cook fish on heated oiled grill plate until just cooked.
3 Serve fish with salsa.
salsa combine ingredients in medium bowl.

preparation time 15 minutes **cooking time** 10 minutes **serves** 4
nutritional count per serving 4.6g total fat (1.4g saturated fat);
953kJ (228 cal); 3.2g carbohydrate; 42.2g protein; 1.7g fibre

Devilled squid

You need to soak 12 bamboo skewers in cold water for at least an hour before use to prevent them from splintering or burning during cooking.

2 large squid hoods (500g)
¼ cup finely chopped fresh mint
marinade
2 teaspoons finely grated lemon rind
¼ cup (60ml) lemon juice
1 tablespoon peanut oil
2 cloves garlic, crushed
2 teaspoons Tabasco sauce
lime vinaigrette
2 teaspoons white sugar
2 tablespoons lime juice
⅓ cup (80ml) peanut oil
2 cloves garlic, crushed
2 green onions, chopped finely
1 fresh small red thai chilli, sliced thinly

1 Make marinade.
2 Cut squid hoods in half lengthways, then cut lengthways into 1cm strips; thread onto skewers. Place skewers in large shallow dish, pour over marinade. Cover; refrigerate at least 20 minutes or until required.
3 Drain skewers over small bowl; reserve marinade. Cook skewers on heated oiled grill plate, brushing occasionally with reserved marinade, until just cooked.
4 Meanwhile, make lime vinaigrette.
5 Sprinkle squid with mint and serve with vinaigrette.
marinade combine ingredients in small bowl.
lime vinaigrette place ingredients in screw-top jar; shake well.

preparation time 30 minutes (plus refrigeration time)
cooking time 10 minutes **serves** 4
nutritional count per serving 24.4g total fat (4.6g saturated fat); 1342kJ (321 cal); 3.4g carbohydrate; 21.4g protein; 0.9g fibre

Oysters with bacon butter

2 rashers rindless bacon (130g), chopped finely
90g butter, softened
1 tablespoon tomato sauce
1 tablespoon worcestershire sauce
2 tablespoons finely chopped fresh flat-leaf parsley
24 medium oysters (600g), on the half shell

1 Cook bacon on heated oiled flat plate, stirring, until crisp; drain on absorbent paper, cool.
2 Beat butter in small bowl until smooth; stir in sauces and parsley. Stir cooled bacon into butter mixture.
3 Place a heaped teaspoon of bacon butter onto each oyster; cook on heated grill plate until butter is melted.

preparation time 10 minutes **cooking time** 5 minutes **serves** 4
nutritional count per serving 23g total fat (13.8g saturated fat); 1154kJ (276 cal); 3.1g carbohydrate; 14.8g protein; 0.3g fibre

Prawn sizzlers

40 uncooked medium prawns (1.8kg)
¼ cup (60ml) peanut oil
2 cloves garlic, crushed
2 tablespoons sambal oelek
1½ tablespoons finely chopped fresh thyme

1 Shell and devein prawns, leaving heads and tails intact. Combine prawns with remaining ingredients in large bowl. Cover; refrigerate at least 20 minutes or until required.
2 Cook prawns on heated oiled grill plate until just cooked.

preparation time 15 minutes (plus refrigeration time)
cooking time 10 minutes **serves** 4
nutritional count per serving 15.1g total fat (2.7g saturated fat); 1388kJ (332 cal); 2.5g carbohydrate; 46.3g protein; 0.3g fibre

Tuna with coriander dressing

4 x 175g tuna steaks
500g baby new potatoes
¼ cup (60ml) olive oil
1 tablespoon lemon juice
1 medium red onion (170g), sliced thinly
¼ cup (30g) pecans, roasted
200g baby spinach leaves
coriander dressing
2 teaspoons coriander seeds
1 clove garlic, peeled
1 cup firmly packed fresh coriander leaves
¼ cup (60ml) olive oil
1 tablespoon lemon juice

1 Make coriander dressing.
2 Rub half the coriander dressing over tuna; cover, refrigerate 1 hour.
3 Boil, steam or microwave potatoes until tender; drain, slice thickly.
4 Cook tuna on a heated oiled grill plate until cooked as desired.
5 Combine remaining coriander dressing with oil and lemon juice.
6 Combine potato, onion, nuts and spinach; divide among serving plates.
Top with tuna and drizzle with remaining coriander mixture.
coriander dressing blend or process ingredients until smooth.

preparation time 45 minutes (plus refrigeration time)
cooking time 20 minutes **serves** 4
nutritional count per serving 43g total fat (8.2g saturated fat);
2826kJ (676 cal); 20.1g carbohydrate; 49.9g protein; 5g fibre
tip you can use lime juice instead of lemon juice, if you prefer.

Whole fish and vegetables with chilli basil butter sauce

4 baby cauliflowers (500g), halved
2 trimmed corn cobs (500g), cut into 2cm rounds
400g baby carrots, trimmed
2 tablespoons olive oil
4 x 240g whole white fish
chilli basil butter sauce
80g butter
2 fresh small red thai chillies, chopped finely
⅓ cup firmly packed fresh basil leaves, shredded finely
1 tablespoon lemon juice

1 Place vegetables and half of the oil in large bowl; toss to combine. Cook vegetables on heated oiled barbecue until browned all over and cooked through.
2 Meanwhile, make chilli basil butter sauce.
3 Score each fish three times both sides; brush all over with remaining oil. Cook fish on heated oiled grilled plate until just cooked.
4 Serve fish and vegetables drizzled with sauce.
chilli basil butter sauce melt butter in small saucepan; stir in chilli, basil and juice until combined.

preparation time 25 minutes **cooking time** 30 minutes **serves** 4
nutritional count per serving 32.2g total fat (13.9g saturated fat); 2608kJ (624 cal); 22.7g carbohydrate; 56.4g protein; 9.3g fibre
tip we used bream in this recipe, but you can use any firm white fish. You can also use fillets instead of a whole fish, if preferred.

Garfish with sweet cucumber and peanut sauce

18 whole garfish (1.5kg), cleaned
cooking-oil spray
sweet cucumber and peanut sauce
¼ cup (55g) caster sugar
½ cup (125ml) water
¼ cup (60ml) lime juice
1 tablespoon fish sauce
2 fresh medium red chillies, sliced thinly
1cm piece fresh ginger (5g), grated
1 lebanese cucumber (130g), peeled, seeded, chopped
1 green onion, sliced thinly
1 tablespoon chopped fresh coriander
1 tablespoon chopped toasted peanuts

1 Make sweet cucumber and peanut sauce.
2 Meanwhile, spray garfish both sides with cooking-oil; cook, in batches, on heated oiled grill plate until browned and cooked through.
3 Serve garfish with sauce and, if desired, thick char-grilled lime slices.
sweet cucumber and peanut sauce cook sugar and the water in small saucepan, stirring, without boiling, until sugar dissolves. Bring to the boil; simmer, uncovered, until syrup is reduced by half. Remove syrup from heat, stir in juice, fish sauce, chilli and ginger; cool. Just before serving, stir in remaining ingredients.

preparation time 15 minutes
cooking time 25 minutes (plus cooling time) **serves** 6
nutritional count per serving 3.6g total fat (3.4g saturated fat);
782kJ (187 cal); 10.3g carbohydrate; 28.3g protein; 0.6g fibre
tip the sweet cucumber and peanut sauce can be made up to four days ahead; store, covered, in the refrigerator.

Grilled chicken thigh fillets with salsa verde and kipfler smash

8 chicken thigh fillets (880g)
600g kipfler potatoes, unpeeled
50g butter, chopped
salsa verde
½ cup coarsely chopped fresh flat-leaf parsley
¼ cup coarsely chopped fresh mint
⅓ cup (80ml) olive oil
½ cup (125ml) lemon juice
¼ cup (50g) drained capers, chopped coarsely
8 drained anchovy fillets, chopped finely
2 cloves garlic, crushed

1 Make salsa verde.
2 Combine ⅓ cup of the salsa verde and chicken in medium bowl.
3 Cook chicken on heated oiled grill plate until browned both sides and cooked through.
4 Meanwhile, boil, steam or microwave potatoes until tender; drain. Using potato masher, crush potato roughly in large bowl with butter.
5 Serve chicken with potato topped with remaining salsa verde.
salsa verde combine ingredients in small bowl.

preparation time 15 minutes **cooking time** 25 minutes **serves** 4
nutritional count per serving 45.3g total fat (14.3g saturated fat);
2897kJ (693 cal); 22.1g carbohydrate; 47.2g protein; 3.5g fibre

Harissa chicken with rocket and cucumber salad

4 x 500g small chickens
1 tablespoon harissa paste
1 teaspoon finely grated lemon rind
¼ cup (60ml) olive oil
2 teaspoons cumin seeds
1 teaspoon ground coriander
200g yogurt
1 clove garlic, crushed
2 lebanese cucumbers (260g)
150g baby rocket leaves
2 tablespoons lemon juice

1 Rinse chickens under cold water; pat dry inside and out with absorbent paper. Using kitchen scissors, cut along each side of each chicken's backbone; discard backbone. Place chickens, skin-side up, on board; using heel of hand, press down on breastbone to flatten chickens.
2 Combine paste, rind and 1 tablespoon of the oil in large bowl, add chickens; rub mixture all over chickens.
3 Cook chickens on heated oiled grill plate, uncovered, 10 minutes; cover, cook, over low heat, another 10 minutes or until cooked through.
4 Meanwhile, dry-fry spices in small frying pan, stirring, until fragrant. Cool 10 minutes. Combine spices with yogurt and garlic in small bowl.
5 Using vegetable peeler, slice cucumber lengthways into ribbons. Combine cucumber in large bowl with rocket, juice and remaining oil.
6 Serve chickens with yogurt and salad.

preparation time 25 minutes **cooking time** 20 minutes **serves** 4
nutritional count per serving 55.2g total fat (15.4g saturated fat); 3043kJ (728 cal); 4.9g carbohydrate; 52.8g protein; 1.5g fibre
tips a small chicken is also known as spatchcock; no more than 6 weeks old, it weighs a maximum of 500g. Spatchcock is also, a cooking term to describe splitting a small chicken open, then flattening and grilling. Harissa is a North African paste made from dried red chillies, garlic, olive oil and caraway seeds; can be used as a rub for meat, an ingredient in sauces and dressings, or eaten as a condiment. It is available from Middle Eastern food shops and some supermarkets.

Tamarind, orange and honey chicken drumettes

30 chicken drumettes (2kg)
2 teaspoons finely grated orange rind
⅓ cup (80ml) orange juice
⅓ cup (120g) honey
⅓ cup (115g) tamarind concentrate
½ cup (125ml) japanese soy sauce
600g baby buk choy, trimmed, quartered
2 medium red capsicums (400g), sliced thickly
230g fresh baby corn
1 tablespoon tamarind concentrate, extra
2 teaspoons sesame oil

1 Combine drumettes, rind, juice, honey, tamarind and half the sauce in large bowl. Cover; refrigerate 3 hours or overnight.
2 Cook drumettes on heated oiled grill plate, turning and brushing occasionally with marinade, about 30 minutes or until cooked.
3 Meanwhile, cook buk choy, capsicum and corn on heated oiled flat plate until tender. Place vegetables in medium bowl with combined remaining sauce, extra tamarind and oil; toss to combine.
4 Serve chicken with vegetables.

preparation time 15 minutes (plus refrigeration time)
cooking time 30 minutes **serves** 6
nutritional count per serving 22.3g total fat (6.3g saturated fat); 1994kJ (477 cal); 30.8g carbohydrate; 37g protein; 4.1g fibre

Piri piri chicken thigh fillets

2 tablespoons olive oil
1 tablespoon apple cider vinegar
2 teaspoons brown sugar
8 x 125g chicken thigh fillets
piri piri paste
4 fresh long red chillies, chopped coarsely
1 teaspoon dried chilli flakes
2 cloves garlic, quartered
1 teaspoon sea salt

1 Make piri piri paste.
2 Combine paste with oil, vinegar, sugar and fillets in medium bowl.
Cook fillets on heated oiled grill plate until cooked through.
3 Serve chicken with lime, if desired.
piri piri paste using mortar and pestle, grind ingredients to form a paste.

preparation time 10 minutes **cooking time** 15 minutes **serves** 4
nutritional count per serving 27.2g total fat (6.8g saturated fat);
1822kJ (436 cal); 1.8g carbohydrate; 46.6g protein; 0.3g fibre

Tikka chicken pizza

2 medium brown onions (300g), sliced thinly
1 tablespoon brown sugar
400g chicken tenderloins
¼ cup (75g) tikka paste
⅓ cup (110g) mango chutney
4 pieces naan (200g)
⅓ cup (45g) roasted slivered almonds
⅓ cup (95g) yogurt
⅓ cup (50g) raisins
¼ cup loosely packed fresh coriander leaves

1 Combine onion and sugar in small bowl. Cook onion mixture on heated oiled flat plate, turning, about 10 minutes or until mixture caramelises.
2 Meanwhile, slice chicken lengthways into thin strips; combine with paste in medium bowl. Cook chicken on heated oiled grill plate until cooked.
3 Spread chutney over naan; top with onion, chicken strips and nuts.
4 Cook pizzas on hot grill plate about 5 minutes or until bases are browned. Serve topped with yogurt, raisins and coriander.

preparation time 10 minutes **cooking time** 20 minutes **serves** 4
nutritional count per serving 27.2g total fat (8g saturated fat);
2470kJ (591 cal); 55g carbohydrate; 29.1g protein; 6.2g fibre
tip naan is the rather thick, leavened bread associated with the tandoori dishes of northern India, where it is baked pressed against the inside wall of a heated tandoor (clay oven). Now available prepared by commercial bakeries and sold in most supermarkets.

Spiced grilled chicken with tomato chilli sauce

2 teaspoons olive oil
¼ cup (60ml) lemon juice
1 teaspoon ground cumin
2 teaspoons sweet paprika
8 x 125g chicken thigh fillets
tomato chilli sauce
¼ cup (55g) firmly packed brown sugar
¼ cup (60ml) red wine vinegar
2 fresh long red chillies, chopped coarsely
4 large egg tomatoes (360g), chopped coarsely

1 Make tomato chilli sauce.
2 Meanwhile, combine oil, juice, spices and chicken in medium bowl. Cook chicken on heated oiled grill plate until cooked through.
3 Serve chicken with sauce.

tomato chilli sauce cook sugar and vinegar in medium saucepan, stirring, over low heat, until sugar dissolves. Add chilli and tomato; bring to the boil. Reduce heat; simmer, uncovered, 15 minutes. Drain sauce over small bowl; reserve solids. Return liquid to pan; bring to the boil. Boil, uncovered, until liquid is reduced by half. Return tomato solids to pan; stir over heat until sauce is hot.

preparation time 10 minutes **cooking time** 25 minutes **serves** 4
nutritional count per serving 20.4g total fat (5.8g saturated fat); 1747kJ (418 cal); 10.8 carbohydrate; 47.6g protein; 1.1g fibre

Sumac chicken with minted eggplant

1 teaspoon finely grated lemon rind
⅓ cup (80ml) lemon juice
2 teaspoons sumac
2 teaspoons caster sugar
1 tablespoon tahini
800g chicken tenderloins
2 medium eggplants (600g), sliced thickly
¼ cup (60ml) olive oil
½ cup coarsely chopped fresh mint
1 lemon (140g), sliced thickly

1 Combine rind, half the juice, sumac, sugar, tahini and chicken in large bowl.
2 Cook chicken on heated oiled grill plate until cooked. Remove from heat; cover to keep warm.
3 Cook eggplant on cleaned heated oiled grill plate until browned; combine eggplant in medium bowl with remaining juice, oil and mint.
4 Serve chicken and eggplant with lemon slices.

preparation time 10 minutes **cooking time** 15 minutes **serves** 4
nutritional count per serving 28.3g total fat (5.7g saturated fat); 2107kJ (504 cal); 14.2g carbohydrate; 45.9g protein; 5.1g fibre
tips sumac is a purple-red, astringent spice ground from berries growing on shrubs that flourish wild around the Mediterranean; adds a tart, lemony flavour. Can be found in Middle Eastern food stores.
Tahini is a sesame seed paste available from Middle Eastern food stores, many supermarkets and health food stores.

Pesto chicken with grilled zucchini

6 medium zucchini (720g), sliced thickly lengthways
2 tablespoons olive oil
1 clove garlic, crushed
1 tablespoon finely chopped fresh basil
1 teaspoon finely grated lemon rind
⅓ cup (90g) sun-dried tomato pesto
2 tablespoons chicken stock
4 x 200g chicken thigh fillets, cut into thirds

1 Cook zucchini on heated oiled grill plate, in batches, until tender.
Combine with oil, garlic, basil and rind in medium bowl; cover to keep warm.
2 Combine pesto, stock and chicken in large bowl. Cook chicken
on heated oiled grill plate, brushing occasionally with pesto mixture,
until cooked.
3 Serve chicken with zucchini.

preparation time 10 minutes **cooking time** 15 minutes **serves** 4
nutritional count per serving 33.1g total fat (7.6g saturated fat);
2611kJ (481 cal); 3.3g carbohydrate; 41.7g protein; 3.6g fibre

Salt and pepper chicken skewers on baby buk choy

You need to soak 12 bamboo skewers in cold water for at least an hour before use to prevent them from splintering or burning during cooking.

8 chicken thigh fillets (880g), chopped coarsely
1 teaspoon sichuan peppercorns, crushed
½ teaspoon five-spice powder
2 teaspoons sea salt
1 teaspoon sesame oil
600g baby buk choy, quartered
1 tablespoon oyster sauce
1 teaspoon soy sauce
1 tablespoon chopped fresh coriander

1 Thread chicken onto skewers. Combine peppercorns, five-spice and salt in small bowl; sprinkle mixture over chicken, then press in firmly.
2 Cook chicken, in batches, on heated oiled grill plate until browned and cooked through.
3 Meanwhile, heat oil in wok; stir-fry buk choy with combined sauces until just wilted.
4 Divide buk choy among serving plates; top with chicken skewers. Serve sprinkled with coriander.

preparation time 20 minutes **cooking time** 20 minutes **serves** 4
nutritional count per serving 17.4g total fat (5.0g saturated fat);
1438kJ (344 cal); 3.2g carbohydrate; 42.9g protein; 2.1g fibre

Five-spice chicken

750g chicken tenderloins
1 teaspoon peanut oil
1½ teaspoons five-spice powder
2 cloves garlic, crushed
250g hokkien noodles
300g baby corn
500g asparagus
1 medium red capsicum (200g), sliced thinly
¼ cup chopped fresh flat-leaf parsley

1 Combine chicken, oil, five-spice and garlic in medium bowl.
2 Cook chicken, in batches, on heated oiled grill plate until browned and cooked through.
3 Meanwhile, place noodles in medium heatproof bowl; cover with boiling water, separate with fork, drain.
4 Cut baby corn in half. Snap woody ends off asparagus; chop remaining spears into same-sized pieces as halved corn. Stir-fry corn, asparagus and capsicum in heated oiled wok until just tender; add noodles.
5 Stir parsley into vegetables off the heat, then divide mixture among serving dishes; top with chicken.

preparation time 20 minutes **cooking time** 15 minutes **serves** 4
nutritional count per serving 6.8g total fat (1.4g saturated fat);
1689kJ (404 cal); 30.7g carbohydrate; 51.0g protein; 6.7g fibre

Chicken tenderloins in green peppercorn and tarragon dressing

4 medium potatoes (800g)
8 chicken tenderloins (600g)
1 tablespoon cracked black pepper
4 large tomatoes (1kg), sliced thinly
1 medium red onion (170g), sliced thinly
green peppercorn and tarragon dressing
2 tablespoons water
2 teaspoons drained green peppercorns, crushed
2 teaspoons wholegrain mustard
2 green onions, sliced thinly
1 tablespoon chopped fresh tarragon
1 tablespoon olive oil
1 tablespoon caster sugar
⅓ cup (80ml) white wine vinegar

1 Boil, steam or microwave potato until just tender; drain.
2 Meanwhile, coat chicken all over in black pepper; cook, in batches, on heated oiled grill plate until browned and cooked through. Cover; stand 5 minutes, slice thickly.
3 When potatoes are cool enough to handle, slice thickly. Cook potatoes, in batches, on same heated oiled grill plate until browned both sides.
4 Meanwhile, make green peppercorn and tarragon dressing.
5 Arrange chicken, potato, tomato and onion slices on serving plates; drizzle with dressing.
green peppercorn and tarragon dressing whisk ingredients in small bowl.

preparation time 20 minutes (plus standing time)
cooking time 30 minutes **serves** 4
nutritional count per serving 13.4g total fat (3.2g saturated fat); 1797kJ (430 cal); 34.1g carbohydrate; 39.6g protein; 6.6g fibre

Lemon basil chicken on hot potato salad

4 chicken thigh cutlets (640g)
2 cloves garlic, crushed
2 tablespoons lemon juice
1 teaspoon cracked black pepper
½ cup chopped fresh basil
5 slices pancetta (75g)
500g new potatoes, halved
¼ cup (60g) sour cream
¼ cup (75g) mayonnaise
2 tablespoons drained green peppercorns, chopped coarsely
2 tablespoons french dressing

1 Combine thigh cutlets, garlic, juice, pepper and half of the basil in medium bowl.
2 Cook thigh cutlets, in batches, on heated oiled grill plate, brushing occasionally with marinade until browned and cooked through. Cover to keep warm.
3 Cook pancetta on heated oiled grill plate about 1 minute each side or until crisp; chop coarsely.
4 Meanwhile, boil, steam or microwave potato until just tender; drain. Divide potato among serving plates; drizzle with combined sour cream, mayonnaise, peppercorns, dressing, remaining basil and pancetta.
5 Serve chicken with hot potato salad.

preparation time 15 minutes **cooking time** 20 minutes **serves** 4
nutritional count per serving 25.3g total fat (8.3g saturated fat);
1839kJ (440 cal); 23.7g carbohydrate; 28.3g protein; 3.1g fibre

Paprika chicken with raisin and coriander pilaf

8 skinless chicken thigh cutlets (1.3kg)
2 tablespoons lemon juice
3 cloves garlic, crushed
½ teaspoon hot paprika
1 teaspoon sweet paprika
1 teaspoon ground cinnamon
¾ cup (200g) yogurt
1 tablespoon olive oil
1 medium brown onion (150g), chopped finely
2 cups (200g) basmati rice
1 litre (4 cups) chicken stock
½ cup (85g) chopped raisins
¾ cup chopped fresh coriander

1 Combine chicken, juice, garlic and spices in large bowl. Cover; refrigerate 3 hours or overnight.
2 Cook chicken, in batches, on heated oiled grill plate, brushing with a little of the yogurt, until browned and cooked through.
3 Meanwhile, heat oil in medium saucepan; cook onion, stirring, until softened. Add rice; stir to coat in onion mixture. Add stock; bring to the boil. Reduce heat; simmer, covered, stirring occasionally, about 25 minutes or until rice is almost tender. Stir in raisins; cook, covered, 5 minutes.
4 Just before serving, stir coriander into pilaf off the heat. Top pilaf with chicken and remaining yogurt.

preparation time 15 minutes (plus refrigeration time)
cooking time 35 minutes **serves** 4
nutritional count per serving 24.2g total fat (7.4g saturated fat);
2834kJ (678 cal); 61.5g carbohydrate; 52.2g protein; 2.6g fibre

Lamb fillets in sumac with chickpea salad

1 tablespoon sumac
8 lamb fillets (800g)
1 cup (120g) frozen peas
2 x 300g cans chickpeas, rinsed, drained
1 medium red capsicum (200g), chopped finely
1 small red onion (80g), chopped finely
citrus dressing
½ cup (125ml) orange juice
¼ cup (60ml) lemon juice
2 tablespoons olive oil

1 Make citrus dressing.
2 Combine 2 tablespoons of the dressing, sumac and lamb in medium bowl.
3 Cook lamb on heated oiled grill plate, uncovered, until cooked as desired. Cover lamb; stand 5 minutes, slice diagonally.
4 Meanwhile, boil, steam or microwave peas until just tender; drain.
5 Place peas in large bowl with chickpeas, capsicum, onion and ½ cup of the remaining dressing; toss gently to combine.
6 Serve lamb on salad; drizzle with remaining dressing.
citrus dressing place ingredients in screw-top jar; shake well.

preparation time 10 minutes **cooking time** 10 minutes **serves** 4
nutritional count per serving 18.7g total fat (4.8g saturated fat);
1956kJ (468 cal); 21.4g carbohydrate; 49.9g protein; 7.4g fibre
tip sumac is a purple-red, astringent spice ground from berries growing on shrubs that flourish wild around the Mediterranean; adds a tart, lemony flavour. Can be found in Middle Eastern food stores.

Kofta with tunisian carrot salad

500g lamb mince
1 cup (70g) fresh breadcrumbs
¼ cup finely chopped fresh mint
1 teaspoon ground allspice
1 teaspoon ground coriander
1 teaspoon cracked black pepper
1 tablespoon lemon juice
200g yogurt
tunisian carrot salad
3 large carrots (540g)
¼ cup (60ml) lemon juice
1 tablespoon olive oil
½ teaspoon ground cinnamon
½ teaspoon ground coriander
¼ cup firmly packed fresh mint leaves
¼ cup (35g) roasted shelled pistachios
¼ cup (40g) sultanas

1 Using hand, combine mince, breadcrumbs, mint, spices and juice in medium bowl; roll mixture into 12 balls, then into sausage-shaped kofta.
2 Cook kofta on heated oiled flat plate until cooked through.
3 Meanwhile, make tunisian carrot salad.
4 Serve kofta with salad and yogurt.
tunisian carrot salad cut carrot into 5cm pieces; slice pieces thinly lengthways. Cook carrot on heated oiled grill plate until just tender. Place carrot in large bowl with remaining ingredients; toss gently to combine.

preparation time 15 minutes **cooking time** 15 minutes **serves** 4
nutritional count per serving 20g total fat (6.2g saturated fat); 1873kJ (448 cal); 30.0g carbohydrate; 33.8g protein; 6.5g fibre

Balsamic lamb with fattoush

8 lamb loin chops (800g)
¼ cup (60ml) balsamic vinegar
1 tablespoon olive oil
2 cloves garlic, crushed
fattoush
2 large pitta bread
1 lebanese cucumber (130g), seeded, sliced thinly
3 medium tomatoes (450g), seeded, sliced thinly
1 small red onion (100g), sliced thinly
2 green onions, sliced thickly
2 tablespoons olive oil
¼ cup (60ml) lemon juice
1 clove garlic, crushed
½ teaspoon sweet paprika

1 Preheat oven to 220°C/200°C fan-forced; make fattoush.
2 Meanwhile, brush lamb with combined vinegar, oil and garlic; cook on
heated oiled grill plate until cooked as desired. Cover to keep warm.
3 Serve lamb with fattoush.
fattoush toast bread in oven about 5 minutes or until crisp. Place
remaining ingredients in large bowl. Break bread into pieces over salad;
toss gently to combine.

preparation time 20 minutes **cooking time** 15 minutes **serves** 4
nutritional count per serving 27.9g total fat (8.4g saturated fat);
2098kJ (502 cal); 24.6g carbohydrate; 37.3g protein; 3.5g fibre

Rosemary and garlic lamb kebabs

8 x 15cm stalks fresh rosemary
1 clove garlic, crushed
1 tablespoon lemon juice
1 tablespoon olive oil
500g diced lamb

1 Pull enough leaves from base of rosemary stalks to make 2 tablespoons of finely chopped leaves; combine in small bowl with garlic, juice and oil.
2 Thread lamb onto rosemary skewers; brush with rosemary oil mixture.
3 Cook kebabs on heated oiled grill plate until browned all over and cooked as desired.

preparation time 20 minutes **cooking time** 20 minutes **serves** 4
nutritional count per serving 15.6g total fat (5.7g saturated fat); 1024kJ (245 cal); 0.3g carbohydrate; 26.2g protein; 0.1g fibre

Haloumi and allspice lamb kebabs

You need to soak eight bamboo skewers in cold water for at least an hour before use to prevent them from splintering or burning during cooking.

½ teaspoon ground allspice
1 teaspoon cracked black pepper
1 clove garlic, crushed
2 tablespoons lemon juice
2 tablespoons olive oil
500g diced lamb
200g haloumi cheese, cut into 2cm pieces

1 Combine allspice, pepper, garlic, juice, oil and lamb in medium bowl.
2 Thread lamb and cheese, alternately, onto skewers.
3 Cook kebabs on heated oiled grill plate until browned all over and cooked as desired.

preparation time 20 minutes **cooking time** 20 minutes **serves** 4
nutritional count per serving 28.7g total fat (11.8g saturated fat);
1710kJ (409 cal); 1.5g carbohydrate; 36.9g protein; 0.1g fibre

Char-grilled lamb cutlets with white bean puree and tapenade

2 x 400g cans white beans, rinsed, drained
1 cup (250ml) chicken stock
1 clove garlic, crushed
1 tablespoon cream
2 tablespoons lemon juice
2 tablespoons olive oil
¼ cup (60g) black olive tapenade
12 french-trimmed lamb cutlets (600g)
300g baby spinach leaves

1 Combine beans and stock in medium saucepan; bring to the boil. Reduce heat; simmer, uncovered, about 15 minutes or until liquid is absorbed. Transfer to medium bowl; mash beans with garlic, cream, juice and 1 tablespoon of the oil until smooth. Cover to keep warm.
2 Meanwhile, combine tapenade with remaining oil in small bowl.
3 Cook cutlets, in batches, on heated oiled grill plate until browned both sides and cooked as desired. Cover to keep warm.
4 Boil, steam or microwave spinach until just wilted; drain.
5 Divide bean puree, spinach and cutlets among serving plates; spoon tapenade mixture on cutlets.

preparation time 20 minutes **cooking time** 25 minutes **serves** 4
nutritional count per serving 25.6g total fat (9g saturated fat); 1438kJ (344 cal); 8g carbohydrate; 21.1g protein; 5g fibre

Chilli and paprika seared lamb steak with tabbouleh

1 clove garlic, crushed
1 teaspoon dried chilli flakes
1 tablespoon sweet paprika
2 teaspoons ground coriander
1 teaspoon ground cumin
1 tablespoon finely chopped fresh mint
2 tablespoons hot water
4 x 150g lamb steaks
tabbouleh
¼ cup (40g) burghul
2½ cups coarsely chopped fresh flat-leaf parsley
½ cup coarsely chopped fresh mint
½ cup coarsely chopped fresh coriander
3 medium tomatoes (450g), seeded, chopped coarsely
1 medium red onion (170g), chopped finely
⅔ cup (160ml) lemon juice
⅔ cup (160ml) olive oil

1 Make tabbouleh.
2 Combine garlic, spices, mint, the water and steaks in medium bowl.
3 Cook steaks on heated oiled grill plate until browned both sides and cooked as desired. Cover steaks; stand 5 minutes.
4 Serve lamb with tabbouleh.
tabbouleh cover burghul with cold water in small bowl; stand about 10 minutes or until burghul softens, drain. Using hands, squeeze out excess water then combine burghul in medium bowl with herbs, tomato and onion. Place juice and oil in screw-top jar; shake well. Drizzle dressing over tabbouleh; toss gently to combine.

preparation time 30 minutes (plus standing time)
cooking time 10 minutes **serves** 4
nutritional count per serving 44g total fat (8.4g saturated fat); 2195kJ (525 cal); 11.5g carbohydrate; 20.8g protein; 6.4g fibre

Za'atar-crusted lamb kebabs with hummus

You need to soak eight bamboo skewers in cold water for at least an hour before use to prevent them from splintering or burning during cooking.

1 tablespoon olive oil
1 tablespoon lemon juice
800g diced lamb
½ cup coarsely chopped fresh flat-leaf parsley
8 pieces lavash
200g yogurt
hummus
2 x 300g cans chickpeas, rinsed, drained
1 clove garlic, quartered
½ cup (140g) tahini
½ cup (125ml) lemon juice
½ cup (125ml) water
za'atar
1 tablespoon sumac
1 tablespoon toasted sesame seeds
1 teaspoon dried marjoram
2 teaspoons dried thyme

1 Combine oil, juice and lamb in medium bowl. Thread lamb onto skewers.
2 Make hummus. Cover; refrigerate until required.
3 Make za'atar; spread on tray. Roll kebabs in za'atar until coated all over.
4 Cook kebabs on heated oiled grill plate until cooked as desired.
5 Serve kebabs on lavash with hummus, parsley and yogurt.
hummus blend or process ingredients until smooth.
za'atar combine ingredients in small bowl.

preparation time 20 minutes **cooking time** 15 minutes **serves** 4
nutritional count per serving 41.1g total fat (8.5g saturated fat);
4393kJ (1051 cal); 89.7g carbohydrate; 72.8g protein; 14.2g fibre
tips tahini is a sesame seed paste available from Middle Eastern food stores, many supermarkets and health food stores.
While za'atar is easy to make, it can also be purchased in Middle Eastern food shops and some delicatessens.

Tandoori lamb cutlets with fresh coconut and melon chutney

¼ cup (75g) tandoori paste
¼ cup (70g) yogurt
12 french-trimmed lamb cutlets (600g)
fresh coconut and melon chutney
1 cup (110g) coarsely grated fresh coconut
½ large firm honeydew melon (850g), grated coarsely, drained
2 tablespoons finely chopped fresh mint
1 tablespoon lemon juice

1 Combine paste, yogurt and cutlets in large bowl.
2 Cook cutlets on heated oiled grill plate until browned both sides and cooked as desired.
3 Meanwhile, make fresh coconut and melon chutney.
4 Serve cutlets with chutney and, if desired, pappadums and lemon wedges.
fresh coconut and melon chutney combine ingredients in medium bowl.

preparation time 15 minutes **cooking time** 10 minutes **serves** 4
nutritional count per serving 27.3g total fat (13.5g saturated fat); 1601kJ (383 cal); 13.2g carbohydrate; 18.9g protein; 5.7g fibre
tips if fresh coconut is unavailable, use 1 cup finely shredded dried coconut. The chutney is best if made with a firm (just underripe) honeydew melon. To open a fresh coconut, pierce one of the eyes then roast coconut briefly in a very hot oven only until cracks appear in the shell. Cool, then break the coconut apart and grate or flake the firm white flesh.

Lamb burgers with beetroot relish and yogurt

500g lamb mince
1 small brown onion (80g), chopped finely
2 cloves garlic, crushed
1 teaspoon ground cumin
1 egg, beaten lightly
1 tablespoon olive oil
¾ cup (210g) greek-style yogurt
½ teaspoon ground cumin, extra
1 tablespoon finely chopped fresh mint
1 long loaf turkish bread
50g baby rocket leaves
beetroot relish
4 medium beetroot (700g), trimmed, grated coarsely
1 small brown onion (80g), chopped finely
⅓ cup (80ml) water
½ cup (110g) white sugar
⅔ cup (160ml) apple cider vinegar

1 Make beetroot relish.
2 Meanwhile, using hand, combine lamb, onion, garlic, cumin and egg in medium bowl; shape mixture into four patties.
3 Heat oil in large frying pan; cook patties, uncovered, until browned both sides and cooked through. Cover to keep warm.
4 Combine yogurt, extra cumin and mint in small bowl.
5 Cut bread into quarters; halve quarters horizontally. Toast bread, cut-side up. Sandwich rocket, patties, yogurt mixture and relish between bread.
beetroot relish cook beetroot, onion and the water in large frying pan, covered, about 15 minutes or until beetroot is tender. Stir in sugar and vinegar; cook, covered, stirring occasionally, 20 minutes. Uncover; cook, stirring occasionally, 10 minutes or until liquid evaporates.

preparation time 30 minutes **cooking time** 45 minutes **serves** 4
nutritional count per serving 22g total fat (7.9g saturated fat);
3173kJ (759 cal); 95.9g carbohydrate; 43.6g protein; 8.6g fibre
tip beetroot relish will keep, covered and refrigerated, up to three days.

Lemon and garlic lamb kebabs with greek salad

8 x 15cm stalks fresh rosemary
800g lamb fillets, cut into 3cm pieces
3 cloves garlic, crushed
2 tablespoons olive oil
2 teaspoons finely grated lemon rind
1 tablespoon lemon juice
greek salad
5 medium egg tomatoes (375g), cut into wedges
2 lebanese cucumbers (260g), halved lengthways, sliced thinly
1 medium red capsicum (200g), cut into 2cm pieces
1 medium green capsicum (200g), cut into 2cm pieces
1 medium red onion (170g), sliced thinly
¼ cup (40g) seeded kalamata olives
200g fetta cheese, cut into 2cm pieces
2 teaspoons fresh oregano leaves
¼ cup (60ml) olive oil
2 tablespoons apple cider vinegar

1 Remove leaves from bottom two-thirds of each rosemary stalk; sharpen trimmed ends to a point. Thread lamb onto rosemary skewers.
2 Combine garlic, oil, rind and juice; brush kebabs with garlic oil mixture. Cover; refrigerate until required.
3 Make greek salad.
4 Cook kebabs on heated oiled grill plate, brushing frequently with remaining garlic mixture, until cooked. Serve with greek salad.
greek salad place ingredients in large bowl; toss gently to combine.

preparation time 25 minutes **cooking time** 5 minutes **serves** 4
nutritional count per serving 52.5g total fat (18.9g saturated fat); 3085kJ (738 cal); 11.2g carbohydrate; 54.1g protein; 4.1g fibre

Butterflied lamb with fresh mint sauce

Ask your butcher to butterfly the leg of lamb for you.

½ cup (90g) honey
1 tablespoon wholegrain mustard
2kg butterflied leg of lamb
¼ cup loosely packed fresh rosemary sprigs
mint sauce
½ cup (125ml) water
½ cup (110g) firmly packed brown sugar
1 ½ cups (375ml) apple cider vinegar
½ cup finely chopped fresh mint

1 Make mint sauce.
2 Combine a quarter of the mint sauce, honey, mustard and lamb in large shallow dish. Cover; refrigerate 3 hours or overnight, turning occasionally. Refrigerate remaining mint sauce, separately.
3 Drain lamb; place, fat-side down, on heated oiled grill plate. Cover lamb loosely with foil; cook about 10 minutes or until browned underneath. Uncover; turn lamb, sprinkle with rosemary. Cook lamb, covered, about 10 minutes or until cooked as desired (or cook by indirect heat in covered barbecue following manufacturer's instructions). Remove lamb from heat; stand, covered, 15 minutes.
4 Slice lamb thinly; serve with remaining mint sauce, and a tomato and radish salad, if desired.
mint sauce stir the water and sugar in small saucepan over heat, without boiling, until sugar dissolves. Bring to the boil; reduce heat, simmer, uncovered, without stirring, about 5 minutes or until syrup thickens slightly. Combine sugar syrup, vinegar and mint in small bowl.

preparation time 15 minutes (plus refrigeration and standing time)
cooking time 25 minutes **serves** 10
nutritional count per serving 8.1g total fat (3.6g saturated fat); 1166kJ (279 cal); 18.2g carbohydrate; 32.9g protein; 0.2g fibre
tip the mint sauce can be made several days ahead.

Lamb chops with capsicum mayonnaise and fetta and olive mash

100g roasted capsicum
½ cup (150g) whole-egg mayonnaise
8 lamb mid-loin chops (800g)
fetta and olive mash
1kg potato, chopped coarsely
⅔ cup (160ml) warmed buttermilk
200g fetta cheese, crumbled
½ cup (60g) black olives, sliced thinly
1 tablespoon olive oil

1 Blend or process capsicum and mayonnaise until smooth.
2 Make fetta and olive mash.
3 Meanwhile, cook lamb, in batches, on heated oiled grill plate until browned all over and cooked as desired.
4 Serve lamb with capsicum mayonnaise and mash.
fetta and olive mash boil, steam or microwave potato until tender; drain. Mash potato in large bowl with buttermilk until combined. Stir in cheese and olives then drizzle with oil.

preparation time 15 minutes **cooking time** 20 minutes **serves** 4
nutritional count per serving 49.7g total fat (19.5g saturated fat);
3420kJ (818 cal); 43.3g carbohydrate; 47.5g protein; 4.2g fibre

Souvlakia with tomato, almond and mint salad

You need to soak eight bamboo skewers in cold water for at least an hour before use to prevent them from splintering or burning during cooking.

¼ cup (60ml) olive oil
2 teaspoons finely grated lemon rind
¼ cup (60ml) lemon juice
¼ cup finely chopped fresh oregano
800g lamb fillets, cut into 3cm pieces
2 medium yellow capsicums (400g), chopped coarsely
1 medium red onion (150g), chopped coarsely
2 large tomatoes (440g), chopped coarsely
¼ cup (35g) roasted slivered almonds
1 cup firmly packed fresh mint leaves

1 Place oil, rind, juice and oregano in screw-top jar; shake well.
2 Thread lamb, capsicum and onion, alternately, on skewers. Place on baking tray; drizzle with half the dressing.
3 Cook souvlakia on heated oiled grill plate until cooked as desired.
4 Meanwhile, combine tomato, nuts and mint with remaining dressing in small bowl.
5 Serve souvlakia with salad and, if desired, pitta bread.

preparation time 20 minutes **cooking time** 15 minutes **serves** 4
nutritional count per serving 26.1g total fat (5.5g saturated fat); 1914kJ (458 cal); 7.8g carbohydrate; 46.2g protein; 4.3g fibre

Italian mixed grill

Ask your butcher to slice the lamb liver thinly for you. Liver should be cooked quickly as overcooking toughens its delicate texture.

4 french-trimmed lamb cutlets (300g)
3 lamb fillets (300g)
1 teaspoon cracked black pepper
2 tablespoons olive oil
4 thin lamb sausages (320g)
4 small egg tomatoes (240g), halved
4 medium flat mushrooms (320g)
4 baby eggplants (320g), halved lengthways
8 baby brown onions (200g), halved
2 cloves garlic, crushed
200g piece lamb liver, sliced thinly
2 tablespoons plain flour
2 tablespoons balsamic vinegar
1 tablespoon fresh oregano leaves

1 Combine cutlets and fillets in large bowl with pepper and half of the oil.
2 Cook cutlets, fillets and sausages on heated oiled grill plate until cooked as desired. Cover to keep warm.
3 Combine tomato, mushrooms, eggplant, onion and garlic with remaining oil in large bowl. Cook vegetables on heated grill plate until browned and just tender.
4 Meanwhile, toss liver in flour; shake off excess. Cook liver on heated oiled flat plate until cooked as desired.
5 Serve meat with vegetables, sprinkled with vinegar then oregano.

preparation time 15 minutes **cooking time** 20 minutes **serves** 4
nutritional count per serving 42.9g total fat (16.1g saturated fat);
2746kJ (657 cal); 14.9g carbohydrate; 49.5g protein; 8.8g fibre

Harissa lamb cutlets with grilled corn and garlic

¼ cup (75g) harissa
2 tablespoons olive oil
12 lamb cutlets (900g)
4 fresh corn cobs (1.5kg), husks on
4 bulbs garlic
harissa butter
80g butter, softened
3 teaspoons harissa

1 Combine harissa, oil and cutlets in large bowl. Cover; refrigerate overnight.
2 Carefully pull husk down corn cob, leaving it attached at base. Remove as much silk as possible then bring husk back over cob to cover kernels. Tie each cob with kitchen string to hold husk in place; soak corn overnight in large bowl of water.
3 Make harissa butter.
4 Spread 2 teaspoons of the harissa butter over each garlic bulb; wrap bulbs individually in foil.
5 Drain corn. Cook corn and garlic parcels on heated oiled grill plate about 15 minutes or until corn is cooked as desired and garlic is tender.
6 Meanwhile, cook lamb on heated oiled grill plate until cooked as desired.
7 Spread corn with remaining harissa butter; serve with lamb and garlic.
harissa butter combine ingredients in small bowl.

preparation time 15 minutes (plus refrigeration and cooling time)
cooking time 15 minutes **serves** 4
nutritional count per serving 50.2g total fat (21.7g saturated fat); 3662kJ (876 cal); 56.1g carbohydrate; 38.9g protein; 24.5g fibre
tip harissa is a North African paste made from dried red chillies, garlic, olive oil and caraway seeds; can be used as a rub for meat, an ingredient in sauces and dressings, or eaten as a condiment. It is available from Middle Eastern food shops and some supermarkets.

Steak and aïoli open sandwiches

8 beef fillet steaks (1kg)
4 large egg tomatoes (360g), halved lengthways
1 tablespoon olive oil
4 thick slices ciabatta (140g)
1 tablespoon finely shredded fresh basil
1 tablespoon balsamic vinegar
100g mesclun
aïoli
½ cup (150g) whole-egg mayonnaise
1 clove garlic, crushed

1 Preheat grill.
2 Cook steaks on heated oiled grill plate until cooked as desired.
Cover steaks; stand 5 minutes.
3 Meanwhile, place tomato, cut-side up, on oiled oven tray; drizzle
with oil. Place under hot grill about 10 minutes or until softened.
4 Meanwhile, make aïoli.
5 Toast bread both sides. Spread bread with aïoli; top with steaks and
tomato, sprinkle with basil and vinegar. Serve with mesclun.
aïoli combine ingredients in small bowl.

preparation time 10 minutes **cooking time** 20 minutes **serves** 4
nutritional count per serving 46.7g total fat (10.1g saturated fat);
3031kJ (725 cal); 18g carbohydrate; 58.7g protein; 2.6g fibre

Sausages with caramelised onions, roasted kipflers and mushrooms

750g kipfler potatoes
cooking-oil spray
¼ cup coarsely chopped fresh chives
200g swiss brown mushrooms, sliced thickly
8 thick beef sausages (640g)
2 large red onions (600g), sliced thinly
1 tablespoon balsamic vinegar
1 tablespoon brown sugar

1 Boil, steam or microwave potatoes until just tender; drain. Place potatoes on heated oiled flat plate; spray with oil. Cook potatoes until crisp. Remove from heat; sprinkle with chives.
2 Meanwhile, cook mushrooms and sausages on heated oiled flat plate until mushrooms are browned and sausages are cooked through.
3 Cook onion, stirring, on heated oiled flat plate until soft. Sprinkle with vinegar and sugar; cook, stirring, until onion is caramelised.
4 Divide potatoes, sausages and mushrooms among serving plates; top with onion mixture.

preparation time 10 minutes **cooking time** 25 minutes **serves** 4
nutritional count per serving 41.9g total fat (19.6g saturated fat); 2746kJ (657 cal); 39.0g carbohydrate; 26.8g protein; 10.6g fibre

Char-grilled T-bones with potato pancakes

3 fresh long red chillies, chopped finely
2cm piece fresh ginger (10g), grated
2 cloves garlic, crushed
2 tablespoons olive oil
4 x 300g beef T-bone steaks
4 trimmed corn cobs (1kg)
4 medium potatoes (800g), grated coarsely
50g butter

1 Combine chilli, ginger, garlic, oil and steaks in large bowl.
2 Cook steaks on heated oiled grill plate. Cover steaks; stand 5 minutes.
3 Meanwhile, cook corn, turning occasionally, on heated oiled flat plate until tender.
4 To make potato pancakes, squeeze excess moisture from potato; divide into four portions. Heat half the butter on heated flat plate; cook potato portions, flattening with spatula, until browned both sides.
5 Spread corn with remaining butter; serve with steaks and potato pancakes.

preparation time 20 minutes **cooking time** 30 minutes **serves** 4
nutritional count per serving 33.1g total fat (13g saturated fat); 3118kJ (746 cal); 53.4g carbohydrate; 52.8g protein; 11.4g fibre

Chilli-rubbed hickory-smoked beef rib-eye steaks

1 tablespoon finely grated lemon rind
2 teaspoons chilli powder
2 teaspoons dried thyme
1 teaspoon sweet smoked paprika
2 tablespoons olive oil
2 cloves garlic, crushed
4 x 200g beef rib-eye steaks
100g hickory smoking chips
2 cups (500ml) water

1 Combine rind, chilli, thyme, paprika, oil and garlic in large bowl with steaks. Cover; refrigerate 3 hours or overnight.
2 Soak chips in the water in medium bowl; stand 3 hours or overnight.
3 Place drained chips in smoke box alongside steaks on grill plate. Cook steaks, covered, using indirect heat, about 10 minutes or until cooked.

preparation time 10 minutes (plus refrigeration and standing time)
cooking time 10 minutes **serves** 4
nutritional count per serving 27.3g total fat (8.9g saturated fat); 1726kJ (413 cal); 0.4g carbohydrate; 41.1g protein; 0.7g fibre
tip hickory smoking chips called for here are available at most barbecue supply stores, as are other varieties of wood chips that can also be used to smoke meat on the barbecue.

Cheese-stuffed beef steaks with radicchio salad

4 x 125g beef eye-fillet steaks
80g brie cheese, sliced thickly into 4 pieces
1 small radicchio (150g), trimmed, quartered
1 cup (120g) roasted pecans, chopped coarsely
1 large pear (330g), unpeeled, sliced thickly
1 cup loosely packed fresh flat-leaf parsley leaves
¼ cup (60ml) olive oil
2 tablespoons lemon juice

1 Slice steaks in half horizontally. Sandwich cheese slices between steak halves; tie with kitchen string to secure.
2 Cook steaks on heated oiled grill plate until cooked.
3 Meanwhile, cook radicchio on grill plate until browned. Place radicchio and remaining ingredients in large bowl; toss gently to combine.
4 Serve steaks with salad.

preparation time 20 minutes **cooking time** 20 minutes **serves** 4
nutritional count per serving 48.1g total fat (9.8g saturated fat); 2596kJ (621 cal); 12g carbohydrate; 34.2g protein; 5.4g fibre
tip we used a triple-cream brie cheese here; you can replace it with the more easily found blue-vein variety, if you prefer, but choose one that's mild and very creamy.

Grilled beef burgers with eggplant and hummus

600g beef mince
2 teaspoons ground cumin
2 cloves garlic, crushed
¼ cup finely chopped fresh coriander
4 baby eggplants (240g), sliced thickly
3 medium egg tomatoes (225g), sliced thickly
1 medium brown onion (150g), sliced thinly
8 slices sourdough bread (560g)
½ cup (130g) hummus
2 teaspoons lemon juice
1 teaspoon olive oil
100g rocket, trimmed

1 Combine mince, cumin, garlic and coriander in medium bowl; shape mixture into four patties.
2 Cook patties, eggplant, tomato and onion, in batches, on heated oiled grill plate until patties are cooked through and eggplant is tender.
3 Grill bread on same cleaned grill plate until browned both sides.
4 Meanwhile, combine hummus, juice and oil in small bowl.
5 Sandwich rocket, eggplant, patties, tomato, hummus mixture and onion between bread slices.

preparation time 15 minutes   **cooking time** 10 minutes   **serves** 4
nutritional count per serving   21.2g total fat (6.2g saturated fat); 2913kJ (697 cal); 71.6g carbohydrate; 48.1g protein; 12.6g fibre

Chilli and honey barbecued steak with coleslaw

2 tablespoons barbecue sauce
1 tablespoon worcestershire sauce
1 tablespoon honey
1 fresh long red chilli, chopped finely
1 clove garlic, crushed
4 x 200g new-york cut beef steaks
coleslaw
2 cups (160g) finely shredded white cabbage
1 cup (80g) finely shredded red cabbage
1 medium carrot (120g), grated coarsely
3 green onions, sliced thinly
2 tablespoons mayonnaise
1 tablespoon white wine vinegar

1 Combine sauces, honey, chilli, garlic and steaks in large bowl.
2 Cook steaks on heated oiled grill plate until browned both sides and cooked as desired.
3 Make coleslaw; serve with steaks.
coleslaw place cabbages, carrot and onions in large bowl with combined mayonnaise and vinegar; toss gently to combine.

preparation time 30 minutes **cooking time** 10 minutes **serves** 4
nutritional count per serving 15.2g total fat (5.4g saturated fat);
1605kJ (384 cal); 16.6g carbohydrate; 44g protein; 3.6g fibre

Herbed rib-eye with tapenade mash

4 large potatoes (1.2kg), chopped coarsely
1 tablespoon dried italian herbs
1 clove garlic, crushed
2 tablespoons olive oil
4 x 200g beef rib-eye steaks
½ cup (125ml) cream
2 tablespoons black olive tapenade
60g baby rocket leaves

1 Boil, steam or microwave potato until tender; drain. Cover to keep warm.
2 Meanwhile, combine herbs, garlic, oil and steaks in medium bowl.
3 Cook steaks on heated oiled grill plate, brushing occasionally with herb mixture, until cooked as desired. Remove from heat, cover steaks; stand 5 minutes.
4 Mash potato in large bowl with cream and tapenade; stir in half of the rocket.
5 Serve steaks with mash and remaining rocket.

preparation time 10 minutes **cooking time** 25 minutes **serves** 4
nutritional count per serving 34g total fat (14.3g saturated fat); 2930kJ (761 cal); 41.1g carbohydrate; 54.6g protein; 6.4g fibre

Scotch fillet steaks with caramelised onion and garlic mushrooms

6 beef scotch fillet steaks (1.25kg)
½ cup (125ml) dry red wine
2 tablespoons chopped fresh basil leaves
2 cloves garlic, crushed
20g butter
6 medium red onions (1kg), sliced thinly
⅓ cup (75g) firmly packed brown sugar
¼ cup (60ml) red wine vinegar
6 large flat mushrooms (840g)
2 tablespoons olive oil
1 clove garlic, crushed, extra
1 teaspoon lemon pepper

1 Combine steaks, wine, basil and garlic in large bowl. Cover; refrigerate 3 hours or overnight.
2 Melt butter in large frying pan; cook onion, stirring, until soft and browned. Stir in sugar and vinegar; cook, stirring constantly, about 20 minutes or until onion is well browned and mixture thickened.
3 Brush mushrooms with combined oil, extra garlic and lemon pepper; cook on heated oiled grill plate until tender.
4 Drain steaks; discard marinade. Cook steaks, in batches, on heated oiled grill plate until browned and cooked as desired.
5 Top steaks with mushrooms and caramelised onion.

preparation time 15 minutes (plus refrigeration time)
cooking time 35 minutes **serves** 6
nutritional count per serving 21.5g total fat (7.9g saturated fat); 2023kJ (484 cal); 21.4g carbohydrate; 46.5g protein; 2.5g fibre

Rib-eye steak with vegetables

2 medium red capsicums (400g)
2 small eggplants (460g)
2 medium yellow zucchini (240g)
6 beef scotch fillet steaks (1.25kg)
1 cup (260g) black olive tapenade
1 tablespoon olive oil

1 Quarter capsicums, remove seeds and membranes. Roast under grill or in very hot oven, skin-side up, until skin blisters and blackens. Cover capsicum pieces with plastic or paper for 5 minutes, peel away skin.
2 Cut eggplant into 2cm slices. Cut zucchini, lengthways, into 2cm slices.
3 Cook steaks, in batches, on heated oiled grill plate until browned and cooked as desired; cover to keep warm.
4 Cook capsicum, eggplant and zucchini, in batches, on same grill plate until browned all over and soft.
5 Top steaks with eggplant, zucchini and capsicum. Serve with tapenade; drizzle with oil.

preparation time 20 minutes **cooking time** 30 minutes **serves** 6
nutritional count per serving 21.5g total fat (6.4g saturated fat); 1835kJ (439 cal); 12.3g carbohydrate; 47.5g protein; 3.5g fibre

Veal cutlets with green olive salsa and barbecued kipflers

2 tablespoons olive oil
2 cloves garlic, crushed
1 tablespoon finely chopped fresh oregano
2 teaspoons finely grated lemon rind
1 tablespoon lemon juice
4 x 125g veal cutlets
barbecued kipflers
1.5kg kipfler potatoes
2 cloves garlic, crushed
¼ cup fresh thyme leaves
1 tablespoon coarsely grated lemon rind
⅓ cup (80ml) olive oil
¼ cup (60ml) lemon juice
green olive salsa
1 tablespoon lemon juice
¼ cup coarsely chopped fresh flat-leaf parsley
½ cup (80g) finely chopped large green olives
1 small green capsicum (150g), chopped finely
1 tablespoon olive oil
1 clove garlic, crushed
1 tablespoon finely chopped fresh oregano

1 Make barbecued kipflers.
2 Meanwhile, make green olive salsa.
3 Combine oil, garlic, oregano, rind and juice in small bowl; brush mixture over veal. Cook veal on heated oiled grill plate until browned both sides and cooked as desired.
4 Serve veal with kipflers and salsa.
barbecued kipflers boil, steam or microwave potatoes until tender; drain. Halve potatoes lengthways, place in large bowl with combined remaining ingredients; toss to combine. Cook on heated oiled grill plate about 15 minutes or until browned.
green olive salsa combine ingredients in small bowl.

preparation time 25 minutes **cooking time** 30 minutes **serves** 4
nutritional count per serving 35g total fat (5.3g saturated fat);
2897kJ (693 cal); 55.9g carbohydrate; 32.6g protein; 9.1g fibre

Char-grilled veal cutlets and vegetables with tomato and caper salsa

6 baby eggplant (360g), halved lengthways
6 small zucchini (540g), halved lengthways
2 tablespoons olive oil
12 veal cutlets (2kg)
1 tablespoon cracked black pepper
1 tablespoon fresh baby basil leaves
tomato and caper salsa
2 medium tomatoes (300g), seeded, chopped finely
1 small red onion (100g), chopped finely
1 clove garlic, crushed
2 tablespoons drained baby capers, rinsed
1 tablespoon olive oil
1 tablespoon balsamic vinegar

1 Cook eggplant and zucchini, in batches, on heated oiled grill plate until browned and tender, brushing with oil. Cover to keep warm.
2 Sprinkle cutlets with pepper; cook on same heated grill plate until cooked as desired.
3 Meanwhile, make tomato and caper salsa.
4 Serve cutlets with eggplant, zucchini and salsa sprinkled with basil.
tomato and caper salsa combine ingredients in small bowl.

preparation time 15 minutes **cooking time** 20 minutes **serves** 6
nutritional count per serving 15.7g total fat (3.2g saturated fat); 1722kJ (412 cal); 4.5g carbohydrate; 62.3g protein; 3.4g fibre

Veal chops and grilled fennel and mandarin

4 x 200g veal chops
2 baby fennel bulbs (260g), trimmed, halved lengthways
4 small mandarins (400g), peeled, halved horizontally
salsa verde
¼ cup finely chopped fresh flat-leaf parsley
¼ cup finely chopped fresh mint
1 tablespoon finely chopped fennel tips
¼ cup finely chopped fresh chives
1 tablespoon wholegrain mustard
2 tablespoons lemon juice
2 tablespoons drained baby capers, rinsed, chopped finely
1 clove garlic, crushed
⅓ cup (80ml) olive oil

1 Cook chops on heated oiled grill plate until cooked as desired.
2 Cook fennel and mandarin on same grill plate until just browned.
3 Make salsa verde.
4 Serve chops with fennel and mandarin, and topped with salsa verde.
salsa verde combine ingredients in small bowl.

preparation time 25 minutes **cooking time** 20 minutes **serves** 4
nutritional count per serving 21.6g total fat (3.5g saturated fat);
1492kJ (357 cal); 8.4g carbohydrate; 30.4g protein; 3.3g fibre

Veal cutlets with anchovy garlic butter

1 medium lemon (140g)
2 cloves garlic, crushed
1 tablespoon fresh sage leaves
¼ cup (60ml) olive oil
8 veal cutlets (1kg)
anchovy garlic butter
4 drained anchovy fillets, chopped finely
1 clove garlic, crushed
125g butter, softened
1 teaspoon finely chopped fresh sage

1 Peel rind thinly from lemon; cut rind into long, thin strips. Combine rind with garlic, sage, oil and veal in large bowl. Cover; refrigerate 3 hours or overnight.
2 Make anchovy garlic butter.
3 Cook cutlets on heated oiled grill plate until cooked as desired.
4 Serve cutlets with anchovy garlic butter.
anchovy garlic butter combine ingredients in small bowl.

preparation time 10 minutes (plus refrigeration time)
cooking time 10 minutes **serves** 4
nutritional count per serving 45.6g total fat (26.6g saturated fat); 2554kJ (611 cal); 0.8g carbohydrate; 50g protein; 0.9g fibre

Fennel-flavoured veal chops with garlic mustard butter

2 teaspoons fennel seeds
1 teaspoon sea salt
½ teaspoon cracked black pepper
2 tablespoons olive oil
4 x 200g veal chops
4 flat mushrooms (320g)
80g baby rocket leaves
garlic mustard butter
80g butter, softened
1 tablespoon coarsely chopped fresh flat-leaf parsley
1 clove garlic, crushed
1 tablespoon wholegrain mustard

1 Using mortar and pestle, crush seeds, salt and pepper coarsely; stir in oil. Rub mixture all over chops.
2 Cook chops and mushrooms on heated oiled grill plate until browned both sides and cooked as desired.
3 Meanwhile, make garlic mustard butter.
4 Divide rocket among serving plates; top each with mushroom, chops then butter.
garlic mustard butter combine ingredients in small bowl.

preparation time 10 minutes **cooking time** 15 minutes **serves** 4
nutritional count per serving 29.7g total fat (13.2g saturated fat); 1831kJ (438 cal); 2.1g carbohydrate; 39.9g protein; 2.7g fibre

Balsamic rosemary grilled veal steaks

2 tablespoons olive oil
2 tablespoons balsamic vinegar
1 tablespoon fresh rosemary leaves
2 cloves garlic, crushed
4 x 125g veal steaks
4 medium egg tomatoes (300g), halved
4 flat mushrooms (320g)

1 Combine oil, vinegar, rosemary, garlic and steaks in medium bowl.
2 Cook steaks on heated oiled grill plate, brushing occasionally with vinegar mixture, until cooked as desired. Remove from heat; cover to keep warm.
3 Cook tomato and mushrooms on heated oiled grill plate until tender.
4 Serve steaks with grilled vegetables.

preparation time 10 minutes **cooking time** 15 minutes **serves** 4
nutritional count per serving 11.3g total fat (1.8g saturated fat); 1016kJ (243 cal); 2.1g carbohydrate; 31.6g protein; 3.3g fibre

Glazed pork cutlets with celeriac salad

2 teaspoons honey
1 teaspoon dijon mustard
1 tablespoon olive oil
4 pork cutlets (1kg)
400g baby carrots, trimmed
celeriac salad
650g celeriac, grated coarsely
⅓ cup (100g) whole-egg mayonnaise
1 clove garlic, crushed
⅓ cup (80g) light sour cream
2 tablespoons lemon juice
½ cup coarsely chopped fresh flat-leaf parsley
2 teaspoons dijon mustard

1 Whisk honey, mustard and oil in large bowl, add cutlets; toss to coat in mixture.
2 Cook cutlets on heated oiled grill plate until cooked as desired. Cover cutlets; stand 5 minutes.
3 Meanwhile, boil, steam or microwave carrots until just tender; drain. Cover to keep warm.
4 Make celeriac salad.
5 Serve cutlets with salad and carrots.
celeriac salad combine ingredients in medium bowl.

preparation time 5 minutes **cooking time** 15 minutes **serves** 4
nutritional count per serving 37.8g total fat (9.6g saturated fat); 2441kJ (584 cal); 15.5g carbohydrate; 45.6g protein; 9g fibre

Pork cutlets with fennel relish and crushed herbed potatoes

2 tablespoons apple cider vinegar
¼ cup (60ml) olive oil
1 tablespoon dijon mustard
2 teaspoons white sugar
4 x 200g pork loin cutlets
fennel relish
1 large unpeeled green apple (200g), chopped finely
1 small red onion (100g), chopped finely
1 medium fennel bulb (300g), trimmed, chopped finely
crushed herbed potatoes
1kg new potatoes, unpeeled
½ cup (120g) sour cream
40g butter, softened
2 tablespoons coarsely chopped fresh dill
¼ cup coarsely chopped fresh flat-leaf parsley

1 Whisk vinegar, oil, mustard and sugar in medium bowl; place
2 tablespoons of dressing in large bowl. Reserve remaining dressing
for fennel relish.
2 Place cutlets in large bowl; turn to coat in dressing.
3 Meanwhile, make fennel relish and crushed herbed potatoes.
4 Cook drained cutlets on heated oiled grill plate until browned both
sides and cooked through, brushing with dressing occasionally.
5 Serve cutlets with relish and potatoes.
fennel relish combine ingredients in medium bowl with reserved dressing.
crushed herbed potatoes boil, steam or microwave potatoes until
tender; drain. Mash half the potatoes with sour cream and butter in
large bowl until smooth; stir in dill and parsley. Roughly crush remaining
potatoes until skins burst; stir into herbed mash.

preparation time 20 minutes **cooking time** 20 minutes **serves** 4
nutritional count per serving 16g total fat (2.7g saturated fat);
1283kJ (307 cal); 9.4g carbohydrate; 30.2g protein; 2.4g fibre

Chinese barbecued pork

1kg pork scotch fillet
marinade
2 star anise, crushed
2 tablespoons light soy sauce
2 tablespoons brown sugar
1½ tablespoons honey
1½ tablespoons dry sherry
2 teaspoons hoisin sauce
2cm piece fresh ginger (10g), grated
1 clove garlic, crushed
2 green onions, chopped finely
few drops red food colouring

1 Cut pork into quarters lengthways.
2 Combine ingredients for marinade in large shallow dish with pork. Cover; refrigerate 3 hours or overnight.
3 Drain pork; reserve marinade. Cook pork on heated oiled barbecue until browned and cooked through, brushing with reserved marinade during cooking.

preparation time 15 minutes (plus refrigeration time)
cooking time 15 minutes **serves** 6
nutritional count per serving 13.5g total fat (4.5g saturated fat); 1321kJ (316 cal); 11.3g carbohydrate; 35.9g protein; 0.4g fibre

Barbecued pork spareribs with red cabbage coleslaw

2kg slab american-style pork spareribs
barbecue sauce
1 cup (250ml) tomato sauce
¾ cup (180ml) cider vinegar
2 tablespoons olive oil
¼ cup (60ml) worcestershire sauce
⅓ cup (75g) firmly packed brown sugar
2 tablespoons american mustard
1 teaspoon cracked black pepper
2 fresh small red thai chillies, chopped finely
2 cloves garlic, crushed
2 tablespoons lemon juice
red cabbage coleslaw
½ cup (120g) sour cream
¼ cup (60ml) lemon juice
2 tablespoons water
½ small red cabbage (600g), shredded finely
3 green onions, sliced thinly

1 Make barbecue sauce; cool 10 minutes.
2 Place ribs in large shallow baking dish; pour barbecue sauce over ribs. Cover; refrigerate 3 hours or overnight, turning ribs occasionally.
3 Make red cabbage coleslaw.
4 Drain ribs; reserve sauce. Cook ribs on heated oiled grill plate, brushing occasionally with reserved sauce, until cooked.
5 Bring remaining sauce to the boil in small saucepan; boil 4 minutes or until sauce thickens slightly.
6 Cut ribs into serving-sized pieces; serve with hot sauce and coleslaw.
barbecue sauce bring ingredients in medium saucepan to the boil.
red cabbage coleslaw place sour cream, juice and the water in screw-top jar; shake well. Place cabbage and onion in large bowl with dressing; toss gently to combine.

preparation time 15 minutes (plus refrigeration time)
cooking time 25 minutes **serves** 4
nutritional count per serving 39.9g total fat (15.2g saturated fat); 3210kJ (768 cal); 44.4g carbohydrate; 53.6g protein; 8g fibre

Plum and star anise pork spareribs with pear, ginger and chilli salad

2kg slabs american-style pork spareribs
plum and star anise marinade
1 cup (250ml) plum sauce
5cm piece fresh ginger (25g), grated
⅓ cup (80ml) oyster sauce
2 star anise
1 teaspoon dried chilli flakes
pear, ginger and chilli salad
2 medium pears (460g), sliced thinly
2 fresh long red chillies, sliced thinly
2 green onions, sliced thinly
2 cups coarsely chopped fresh mint
2cm piece fresh ginger (10g), grated
2 tablespoons lime juice

1 Make plum and star anise marinade.
2 Place ribs in large shallow baking dish; brush marinade all over ribs. Pour remaining marinade over ribs. Cover; refrigerate 3 hours or overnight, turning ribs occasionally.
3 Drain ribs; reserve marinade. Cook ribs on heated oiled grill plate or until cooked through, turning and brushing frequently with some of the reserved marinade.
4 Meanwhile, make pear, ginger and chilli salad.
5 Boil remaining marinade, uncovered, in small saucepan about 5 minutes or until thickened slightly.
6 Slice ribs into portions; serve with hot marinade and salad.
plum and star anise marinade bring ingredients in medium saucepan to the boil. Remove from heat; cool 10 minutes.
pear, ginger and chilli salad place ingredients in medium bowl; toss gently to combine.

preparation time 25 minutes (plus refrigeration time)
cooking time 30 minutes **serves** 4
nutritional count per serving 18.1g total fat (6.6g saturated fat); 2847kJ (681 cal); 56.3g carbohydrate; 69.6g protein; 5.2g fibre

Pork fillet and pancetta kebabs

8 x 15cm stalks fresh rosemary
600g pork fillet, cut into 2cm pieces
8 slices pancetta (120g), halved
1 large red capsicum (350g), cut into 24 pieces
⅓ cup (80ml) olive oil
1 clove garlic, crushed

1 Remove leaves from bottom two-thirds of each rosemary stalk;
reserve 2 tablespoons leaves, chop finely. Sharpen trimmed ends of
stalks to a point.
2 Wrap each piece of pork in one slice of the pancetta; thread with
capsicum, alternately, onto stalks.
3 Brush kebabs with combined chopped rosemary, oil and garlic.
Cook on heated oiled grill plate, brushing frequently with rosemary
mixture, until cooked.

preparation time 15 minutes **cooking time** 15 minutes **serves** 4
nutritional count per serving 23.6g total fat (4.4g saturated fat);
1601kJ (383 cal); 3.1g carbohydrate; 39.5g protein; 1g fibre

Pork chops with cranberry sauce and kumara cranberry salad

1 tablespoon ground ginger
1 tablespoon ground coriander
1 teaspoon sweet paprika
½ cup (160g) cranberry sauce
2 tablespoons orange juice
2 tablespoons lemon juice
1 tablespoon dijon mustard
4 pork loin chops (1.2kg)
kumara cranberry salad
3 large kumara (1.5kg), cut into 2cm pieces
2 tablespoons olive oil
½ cup (80g) roasted pine nuts
⅓ cup (50g) dried cranberries
1 cup coarsely chopped fresh coriander
¼ cup (60ml) white wine vinegar
2 teaspoons olive oil, extra

1 Combine ginger, coriander, paprika, sauce, juices and mustard in large bowl with chops.
2 Make kumara cranberry salad.
3 Cook chops on heated oiled grill plate, uncovered, until cooked.
4 Serve chops with salad.
kumara cranberry salad boil, steam or microwave kumara until just tender; drain. Combine kumara with oil in large bowl; cook kumara on heated oiled flat plate, uncovered, until browned. Return kumara to same bowl with remaining ingredients; toss gently to combine.

preparation time 15 minutes **cooking time** 30 minutes **serves** 4
nutritional count per serving 48.1g total fat (10.4g saturated fat); 3921kJ (938 cal); 73.3g carbohydrate; 49.3g protein; 8.0g fibre

Five-spice pork belly ribs with crunchy noodle salad

3 cloves garlic, crushed
3cm piece fresh ginger (15g), grated
1½ teaspoons five-spice powder
¼ cup (85g) orange marmalade
¼ cup (90g) honey
2 tablespoons kecap manis
1.5kg pork belly ribs
crunchy noodle salad
¼ cup (60ml) white vinegar
¼ cup (55g) firmly packed brown sugar
¼ cup (60ml) soy sauce
2 teaspoons sesame oil
1 clove garlic, crushed
10 trimmed red radishes (150g), sliced thinly
1 large red capsicum (350g), sliced thinly
½ small wombok (350g), shredded finely
6 green onions, chopped finely
100g packet fried noodles

1 Combine garlic, ginger, five-spice, marmalade, honey and kecap manis in large bowl with ribs. Cover; refrigerate overnight.
2 Drain ribs; reserve marinade. Cook ribs on heated oiled grill plate, uncovered, brushing occasionally with reserved marinade, until cooked through.
3 Meanwhile, make crunchy noodle salad.
4 Serve ribs with salad.
crunchy noodle salad place vinegar, sugar, soy sauce, oil and garlic in screw-top jar; shake well. Place remaining ingredients in large bowl with dressing; toss gently to combine.

preparation time 20 minutes (plus refrigeration time)
cooking time 20 minutes **serves** 4
nutritional count per serving 43.4g total fat (14.6g saturated fat); 3227kJ (772 cal); 57.7g carbohydrate; 36.2g protein; 3.9g fibre

Tex-mex spareribs with grilled corn salsa

2 tablespoons brown sugar
1 tablespoon dried oregano leaves
2 tablespoons sweet paprika
2 teaspoons cracked black pepper
½ teaspoon cayenne pepper
1 tablespoon ground cumin
1 tablespoon garlic powder
¼ cup (60ml) water
2 tablespoons vegetable oil
1.5kg slabs american-style pork spareribs
grilled corn salsa
3 trimmed corn cobs (750g)
2 medium tomatoes (300g), seeded, chopped finely
1 long green chilli, chopped finely
1 medium red onion (170g), chopped finely
1 medium green capsicum (200g), chopped finely
¼ cup coarsely chopped fresh coriander
2 tablespoons lime juice
1 tablespoon olive oil

1 Combine sugar, oregano, spices, the water and oil in large bowl; add ribs, rub spice mixture all over pork.
2 Cook ribs on heated oiled flat plate until cooked.
3 Meanwhile, make grilled corn salsa.
4 Serve ribs with salsa.
grilled corn salsa cook corn on heated oiled grill plate until tender. When cool enough to handle, cut kernels from cobs. Place kernels in medium bowl with remaining ingredients; toss gently to combine.

preparation time 15 minutes **cooking time** 25 minutes **serves** 4
nutritional count per serving 33.7g total fat (9.1g saturated fat); 2508kJ (600 cal); 33.8g carbohydrate; 36.7g protein; 8.3g fibre

Sausages with tomato relish

1 tablespoon olive oil
1 clove garlic, crushed
1 medium brown onion (150g), chopped
2 large tomatoes (500g), chopped coarsely
1 tablespoon balsamic vinegar
1 teaspoon brown sugar
1 tablespoon torn fresh basil leaves
8 thin pork sausages

1 Heat oil in small saucepan, add garlic and onion; cook, stirring, until browned. Add tomato, vinegar and sugar; simmer, uncovered, stirring occasionally, about 20 minutes or until mixture is reduced by half. Just before serving, stir in basil.
2 Meanwhile, cook sausages on heated oiled grill plate until browned and cooked through.
3 Serve sausages with warm tomato relish. Sprinkle with extra basil leaves, if desired.

preparation time 15 minutes **cooking time** 25 minutes **serves** 4
nutritional count per serving 30.5g total fat (11.1g saturated fat); 1576kJ (377 cal); 9.0g carbohydrate; 15.8g protein; 3.6g fibre

Margarita-marinated pork chops with orange and watercress salad

¼ cup (60ml) lime juice
2 fresh small red thai chillies, chopped finely
2 cloves garlic, crushed
½ cup (170g) orange marmalade
⅓ cup finely chopped fresh coriander
½ cup (125ml) tequila
8 pork loin chops (2.2kg)
orange and watercress salad
2 large oranges (600g)
¼ cup (60ml) lime juice
¼ cup (85g) orange marmalade
2 tablespoons olive oil
2 teaspoons tequila
100g watercress, trimmed
1 medium avocado (250g), sliced thinly
½ cup loosely packed fresh coriander leaves

1 Combine juice, chilli, garlic, marmalade, coriander and tequila in large bowl with chops. Cover; refrigerate overnight.
2 Make orange and watercress salad.
3 Drain chops; reserve marinade. Cook chops on heated oiled grill plate brushing occasionally with marinade, until cooked as desired.
4 Serve chops with salad.
orange and watercress salad segment oranges over large bowl; stir in juice, marmalade and oil. Add remaining ingredients; toss gently to combine.

preparation time 15 minutes (plus refrigeration time)
cooking time 15 minutes **serves** 4
nutritional count per serving 57.8g total fat (16.6g saturated fat); 4828kJ (1155 cal); 67.5g carbohydrate; 68.5g protein; 4.4g fibre

Felafel wraps

¾ cup (110g) frozen broad beans, thawed, peeled
420g can chickpeas, rinsed, drained
⅓ cup coarsely chopped fresh flat-leaf parsley
1 small red onion (100g), chopped coarsely
⅓ cup (50g) plain flour
2 teaspoons ground coriander
1 teaspoon ground cumin
1 egg
1 teaspoon bicarbonate of soda
4 large pitta breads (320g)
1 cup (260g) hummus
50g mesclun
marinated grilled eggplant
6 baby eggplants (360g), sliced thinly lengthways
2 tablespoons olive oil
2 cloves garlic, crushed
1 tablespoon white wine vinegar
1 tablespoon finely chopped fresh flat-leaf parsley

1 Blend or process beans, chickpeas, parsley, onion, flour, spices, egg and soda until almost smooth. Shape rounded tablespoons of mixture into 16 felafel patties. Place on tray, cover; refrigerate 30 minutes.
2 Meanwhile, make marinated grilled eggplant.
3 Cook felafel on heated oiled flat plate until browned both sides.
4 Spread heated pittas with hummus; top with mesclun, eggplant and felafel, roll to enclose filling.
marinated grilled eggplant cook eggplant on heated oiled flat plate until browned both sides. Combine eggplant in medium bowl with remaining ingredients.

preparation time 30 minutes (plus refrigeration time)
cooking time 15 minutes **serves** 4
nutritional count per serving 25.5g total fat (4.4g saturated fat); 2738kJ (655 cal); 74.2g carbohydrate; 24.3g protein; 17.1g fibre

Barbecued fennel, orange and red onion with quinoa

5 small fennel bulbs (1kg), trimmed, quartered lengthways
1 large red onion (300g), cut into thick wedges
2 tablespoons olive oil
2 cups (500ml) water
1 cup (170g) quinoa
½ cup (125ml) white wine vinegar
¼ cup coarsely chopped fresh dill
1 medium orange (240g), segmented
1 cup firmly packed fresh flat-leaf parsley leaves

1 Cook fennel and onion on heated oiled grill plate until vegetables are just tender, brushing occasionally with about half of the oil.
2 Meanwhile, bring the water to the boil in small saucepan. Add quinoa; reduce heat, simmer, covered, about 10 minutes or until water is absorbed. Drain.
3 Place fennel, onion and quinoa in large bowl with vinegar, dill, orange, parsley and remaining oil; toss gently to combine.

preparation time 20 minutes **cooking time** 30 minutes **serves** 4
nutritional count per serving 10.2g total fat (1.4g saturated fat);
1208kJ (289 cal); 39.7g carbohydrate; 8.1g protein; 14g fibre
tip quinoa, pronounced keen-wa, is the seed of a leafy plant similar to
spinach. Like corn, rice, buckwheat and millet, quinoa is gluten-free and
thought to be safe for consumption by people with coeliac disease. Its
cooking qualities are similar to rice, and its delicate, slightly nutty taste
and chewy texture make it a good partner for rich or spicy foods. You can
buy it in most health food stores and some delicatessens; keep quinoa
sealed in a glass jar under refrigeration because, like nuts and nut oils,
it spoils easily.

Turkish bread vegetable pizza

1 medium zucchini (120g), sliced thinly
2 baby eggplants (120g), sliced thinly
1 small kumara (250g), sliced thinly
1 medium red capsicum (200g), sliced thickly
200g mushrooms, sliced thickly
1 loaf turkish bread (430g)
⅓ cup (85g) bottled tomato pasta sauce
¼ cup (65g) sun-dried tomato pesto
125g cherry tomatoes, quartered
⅔ cup (100g) seeded kalamata olives
1¼ cups (125g) coarsely grated mozzarella cheese

1 Cook zucchini, eggplant, kumara, capsicum and mushrooms on heated oiled flat plate, uncovered, until tender.
2 Cut bread into quarters; split each piece in half horizontally. Brush cut-side of each bread piece with combined pasta sauce and pesto. Divide grilled vegetables, tomato, olives and cheese among bread pieces.
3 Cook pizzas on heated oiled flat plate, covered, until bases are crisp and cheese melts.

preparation time 15 minutes **cooking time** 20 minutes **serves** 4
nutritional count per serving 17.7g total fat (6.4g saturated fat); 2318kJ (555 cal); 70.3g carbohydrate; 24g protein; 8.2g fibre

Piri-piri vegetables with char-grilled polenta

4 baby eggplants (240g), sliced thickly lengthways
2 medium red onions (340g), cut into wedges
2 large flat mushrooms (200g), sliced thickly
4 large egg tomatoes (360g), quartered, seeded
3 large zucchini (450g), sliced thickly lengthways
1 litre (4 cups) water
1 cup (170g) polenta
50g butter
½ cup (40g) finely grated parmesan cheese
piri-piri marinade
4 fresh small red thai chillies, halved
⅓ cup (80ml) red wine vinegar
2 cloves garlic, quartered
⅓ cup (80ml) olive oil

1 Make piri-piri marinade.
2 Toss eggplant, onion, mushrooms, tomato and zucchini in large bowl with marinade. Cover; refrigerate overnight.
3 Meanwhile, grease deep 19cm-square cake pan. Place the water in medium saucepan; bring to the boil. Gradually add polenta to liquid, stirring constantly. Reduce heat; cook, stirring, about 10 minutes or until polenta thickens. Stir in butter and cheese then spread polenta into prepared pan; cool 10 minutes. Cover; refrigerate overnight.
4 Turn polenta onto board; trim edges. Cut polenta into quarters; cut each quarter in half diagonally to form two triangles. Cook polenta and drained vegetables on heated oiled grill plate about 10 minutes or until polenta is browned and vegetables are tender.
5 Serve polenta triangles with vegetables.
piri-piri marinade blend or process chilli, vinegar and garlic until smooth. With motor operating, gradually add oil in thin, steady stream until mixture thickens.

preparation time 15 minutes (plus refrigeration time)
cooking time 20 minutes **serves** 4
nutritional count per serving 33.4g total fat (11.5g saturated fat); 2203kJ (527 cal); 39.7g carbohydrate; 13.4g protein; 8.3g fibre

Barbecued fetta on greek salad

4 x 100g pieces fetta cheese
2 teaspoons finely chopped fresh oregano
2 teaspoons finely chopped fresh marjoram
2 cloves garlic, chopped finely
1 tablespoon olive oil
4 thick slices sourdough bread (160g)
100g baby spinach leaves
¾ cup (110g) seeded kalamata olives
⅔ cup (100g) drained semi-dried tomatoes
12 drained marinated quartered artichoke hearts (150g)
⅔ cup (110g) drained caperberries, rinsed
2 tablespoons lemon juice

1 Place each piece of cheese on a 20cm-square piece of foil; using fingers, rub combined herbs, garlic and oil gently into cheese. Wrap foil around cheese to enclose.
2 Place foil parcels on heated grill plate; cook about 5 minutes or until cheese is heated through. Toast bread both sides on heated oiled grill plate.
3 Meanwhile, place spinach, olives, tomato, artichokes, caperberries and juice in large bowl; toss gently to combine.
4 Divide salad among serving plates; top with bread and cheese.

preparation time 15 minutes **cooking time** 5 minutes **serves** 4
nutritional count per serving 31.4g total fat (16.4g saturated fat);
2278kJ (545 cal); 36.2g carbohydrate; 25.7g protein; 8.1g fibre

Vegetable salad

1 large red onion (300g)
8 medium egg tomatoes (600g)
8 baby eggplant (480g)
4 medium zucchini (480g)
4 medium yellow patty-pan squash (120g), halved
2 medium red capsicums (400g), sliced thickly
dressing
¼ cup (60ml) extra virgin olive oil
¼ cup (60ml) balsamic vinegar
1 clove garlic, crushed

1 Cut onion and tomatoes into eight wedges each; thinly slice eggplant and zucchini lengthways.
2 Cook onion, tomato, eggplant, zucchini, squash and capsicum, in batches, on heated oiled grill plate until vegetables are browned and just tender.
3 Meanwhile, make dressing.
4 Combine vegetables in large bowl or on serving platter. Drizzle with dressing; toss gently to combine.
dressing place ingredients in screw-top jar; shake well.

preparation time 15 minutes **cooking time** 15 minutes **serves** 8
nutritional count per serving 7.4g total fat (1g saturated fat); 518kJ (124 cal); 8.5g carbohydrate; 3.8g protein; 4.8g fibre

Mushrooms with herb butter

80g butter, melted
1 teaspoon grated lime rind
1 tablespoon lime juice
1 tablespoon chopped fresh flat-leaf parsley
1 tablespoon chopped fresh basil leaves
6 large flat mushrooms (840g)

1 Combine butter, rind, juice and herbs in small bowl.
2 Cook mushrooms on heated oiled grill plate, brushing with half of the butter mixture, until mushrooms are just tender and well browned.
3 Serve mushrooms with remaining butter.

preparation time 5 minutes **cooking time** 10 minutes **serves** 6
nutritional count per serving 11.4g total fat (7.2g saturated fat);
548kJ (131 cal); 0.6g carbohydrate; 5.2g protein; 3.6g fibre

Chilli, tofu and vegetable kebabs

You need to soak 12 bamboo skewers in cold water for at least an hour before use to prevent them from splintering or burning during cooking. We used fiery hot chillies – warn your guests before they eat them!

25 small fresh red thai chillies
⅔ cup (160ml) olive oil
2 teaspoons grated lemon rind
⅓ cup (80ml) lemon juice
1 tablespoon chopped fresh oregano
1 tablespoon chopped fresh dill
2 cloves garlic, crushed
300g packet firm tofu, drained
1 large red onion (300g)
2 medium zucchini (250g)
6 medium yellow patty-pan squash (180g)
12 large cherry tomatoes (250g)

1 Remove and discard seeds from one of the chillies and chop finely. Place oil, rind, juice, herbs, garlic and chopped chilli in screw-top jar; shake well.
2 Cut tofu into 12 even pieces, cut onion into 12 wedges, cut zucchini into 12 pieces and cut each squash in half.
3 Thread a chilli then a piece of zucchini, tofu, tomato, onion, squash and another chilli onto a skewer. Repeat with remaining skewers, chilli, tofu and vegetables.
4 Cook kebabs, in batches, on heated oiled grill plate, brushing with half of the oil mixture, until vegetables are browned on both sides and just tender, turning only once as the tofu is delicate and breaks easily.
5 Serve kebabs with remaining oil mixture.

preparation time 25 minutes **cooking time** 10 minutes **serves** 4
nutritional count per serving 42g total fat (5.9g saturated fat); 1981kJ (474 cal); 10g carbohydrate; 12.6g protein; 5.9g fibre

Chunky black bean and grilled corn salad with cheesy nachos

¾ cup (150g) dried black beans
1 medium red capsicum (200g)
2 trimmed corn cobs (500g)
1 small red onion (100g), chopped finely
1 fresh long red chilli, chopped finely
2 cloves garlic, crushed
1 tablespoon finely grated lime rind
½ cup (125ml) lime juice
1 teaspoon ground cumin
⅓ cup coarsely chopped fresh coriander
2 medium avocados (500g), chopped coarsely
230g packet corn chips
1⅓ cups (160g) coarsely grated cheddar cheese
⅓ cup (80g) sour cream

1 Place beans in medium bowl, cover with water; stand overnight. Rinse under cold water; drain. Cook beans in medium saucepan of boiling water, uncovered, until tender; drain. Rinse under cold water; drain.
2 Quarter capsicum, discard seeds and membranes. Roast under grill, skin-side up, until skin blisters and blackens. Cover capsicum pieces in plastic or paper for 5 minutes; peel away skin, chop capsicum coarsely.
3 Cook corn on heated oiled grill plate until browned lightly and tender; cut kernels from cobs. Combine beans, capsicum, corn, onion, chilli, garlic, rind, juice, cumin and coriander in large bowl. Add avocado; mix gently into salad.
4 Preheat grill.
5 Divide chips and cheese among ovenproof serving plates; grill until cheese melts. Top with salad; serve with sour cream.

preparation time 20 minutes (plus standing time)
cooking time 1 hour **serves** 4
nutritional count per serving 60.2g total fat (25g saturated fat);
4055kJ (970 cal); 67.3g carbohydrate; 31.6g protein; 18.6g fibre

glossary

allspice also called pimento or jamaican pepper.

almonds, slivered tiny pieces cut lengthways.

bacon rashers also called bacon slices.

beans

black also called turtle beans or black kidney beans; an earthy-flavoured dried bean completely different from the better-known Chinese black beans.

broad also called fava, windsor and horse beans; available dried, fresh, canned and frozen. Fresh should be peeled twice (discarding the outer green pod and the beige-green tough inner shell); frozen beans have their pods removed but the beige shell still needs removal.

white a generic term we use for canned or dried cannellini, haricot, navy or great northern beans.

beef

eye fillet tenderloin, fillet.

new york cut boneless striploin (sirloin) steak.

rump boneless tender cut taken from the upper part of the round (hindquarter).

scotch fillet cut from the muscle running behind the shoulder along the spine. Also known as cube roll, cuts include standing rib roast and rib-eye.

beetroot or red beets.

bicarbonate of soda also called baking soda.

breadcrumbs

fresh bread, usually white, processed into crumbs.

packaged prepared fine-textured crunchy white breadcrumbs; good for coating or crumbing foods to be fried.

stale crumbs made by grating, blending or processing 1- or 2-day-old bread.

broccolini a cross between broccoli and Chinese kale; long asparagus-like stems with a long loose floret, both completely edible. Resembles broccoli in looks, but is milder and sweeter in taste.

buk choy also called bok choy, pak choi or chinese white cabbage; has a fresh, mild mustard taste. Both stems and leaves are cooked.

burghul also called bulghur wheat; hulled steamed wheat kernels, once dried, are crushed into various sized grains.

butter we use salted butter.

caperberries olive-sized fruit formed after the buds of the caper bush have flowered; they are usually sold pickled in a vinegar brine with stalks intact.

capers the grey-green buds of a Mediterranean shrub, sold either dried and salted or pickled in a vinegar brine.

capsicum also called pepper or bell pepper.

cardamom a spice native to India and used extensively in its cuisine; can be purchased in pod, seed or ground form. Has an aromatic, sweetly rich flavour.

cashews plump, kidney-shaped, golden-brown nuts with a sweet, buttery flavour; contains 48% fat so should be stored in the refrigerator to avoid becoming rancid. We use roasted unsalted cashews.

cayenne pepper a thin-fleshed, long, extremely hot, dried red chilli, usually ground.

celeriac tuberous root with knobbly brown skin, white flesh and a celery-like flavour.

cheese

blue mould-treated cheeses mottled with blue veining. Varieties include firm and crumbly stilton types and mild, creamy brie-like cheeses.

bocconcini from the diminutive of "boccone", meaning mouthful in Italian; walnut-sized, baby mozzarella, a delicate, semi-soft, white cheese traditionally made from buffalo milk. Sold fresh, it spoils rapidly; store refrigerated in brine, for 1 or 2 days at the most.

brie often referred to in France as the queen of cheeses; soft-ripened cow-milk cheese with a delicate, creamy texture and a rich, sweet taste that varies from buttery to mushroomy. Best served at room temperature after a brief period of ageing, brie should have a bloomy white rind and creamy, voluptuous centre which becomes runny with ripening.

fetta Greek in origin; a crumbly textured goat- or sheep-milk cheese with a sharp, salty taste.

fontina a luscious Italian cheese made from cow milk, has a smooth yet firm texture and a mild, nutty flavour. Ideal for melting or grilling.

haloumi a Greek Cypriot cheese with a semi-firm, spongy texture and very salty yet sweet flavour. It's best grilled or fried, and holds its shape well on being heated. Best eaten while warm as it becomes tough and rubbery on cooling.

mozzarella soft, spun-curd, cow-milk cheese; it is the most popular pizza cheese because of its low melting point and elasticity when heated.

parmesan also called parmigiano; a hard, grainy cow-milk cheese. The curd is salted in brine for a month then aged for up to 2 years.

ricotta a soft, sweet, moist, white cow-milk cheese, low in fat and slightly grainy in texture. Its name roughly

translates as "cooked again" and refers to its manufacture from a whey that is itself a by-product of other cheese making.

chicken

breast fillet breast halved, skinned and boned.

marylands leg and thigh still connected in a single piece; bones and skin intact.

tenderloins thin strip of meat lying just under the breast, especially good for stir-frying.

thigh cutlets thigh with skin and centre bone intact; sometimes found skinned with bone intact.

thigh fillet thigh with skin and centre bone removed.

chickpeas also called garbanzos; an irregularly round legume. Available canned or dried.

chilli

jalapeño pronounced hah-lah-pain-yo. Fairly hot, medium-sized, plump, dark green chilli; available pickled, canned or bottled, and fresh.

pasilla pronounced pah-SEE-yah, also called "chile negro" because of their dark brown colour, are the wrinkled, dried version of fresh chilaca chillies. About 20cm in length, are mildly hot with a rich flavour that adds smoky depth.

red thai also known as "scuds"; tiny, very hot.

sauce, sweet mild, fairly sticky and runny bottled sauce made from red chillies, sugar, garlic and white vinegar; used in Thai cooking and as a condiment.

chinese cooking wine also called hao hsing or chinese rice wine; made from fermented rice, wheat, sugar and salt with a 13.5% alcohol content. Inexpensive and found in Asian food shops; if you can't find it, replace with mirin or sherry.

chorizo sausage Spanish in origin, made of coarsely ground pork and highly seasoned with garlic and chilli.

ciabatta in Italian, the word means slipper, the traditional shape of this popular crisp-crusted, open-textured white sourdough bread.

cinnamon available in pieces (sticks or quills) and in ground form; one of the most common spices. The dried inner bark of the shoots of the Sri Lankan native cinnamon tree; much of what is sold as the real thing is in fact cassia, Chinese cinnamon, from the bark of the cassia tree. Less expensive to process than true cinnamon, it is often blended with Sri Lankan cinnamon to produce the type of "cinnamon" most commonly found in supermarkets.

cloves dried flower buds of a tropical tree; use whole or ground. Strong in scent and taste so use sparingly.

coconut, shredded unsweetened thin strips of dried coconut flesh.

coriander also called cilantro or chinese parsley; bright-green-leafed herb with a pungent aroma and taste. Both stems and roots are used: wash well before chopping. Coriander seeds are dried and sold whole or ground; neither form tastes remotely like the fresh leaf.

cornflour also known as cornstarch.

cos lettuce also called romaine; the traditional caesar salad lettuce. Long, with leaves ranging from dark green on the outside to almost white near the core; the leaves have a stiff centre rib giving a slight cupping effect.

couscous a fine, grain-like cereal product made from semolina. A semolina flour and water dough is sieved then dehydrated to produce minuscule even-sized pellets of couscous; it is rehydrated by steaming or by adding warm liquid. Swells to three or four times its original size.

cucumber, lebanese short, slender and thin-skinned. Probably the most popular variety because of its tender,

edible skin, tiny, yielding seeds, and sweet, fresh and flavoursome taste.

cumin is the dried seed of a plant related to the parsley family. Has a spicy, almost curry-like flavour. Available dried as seeds or ground.

curly endive also called frisée; prickly-looking, curly-leafed green vegetable with an edible white heart. Fairly bitter in flavour; used in salads.

eggplant also called aubergine.

fennel also called finocchio or anise; a crunchy green vegetable slightly resembling celery.

fish sauce called naam pla if Thai-made, nuoc naam if Vietnamese; the two are almost identical. Made from pulverised salted fermented fish; has a pungent smell and strong taste. Use according to your taste.

five-spice powder ingredients vary, but are usually a blend of cloves, ground cinnamon, star anise, sichuan pepper and fennel seeds. Found in most supermarkets or Asian food shops.

flour

plain also known as all-purpose.

rice very fine, almost powdery, gluten-free flour; made from ground white rice.

gai lan also called gai larn, chinese broccoli and chinese kale; green

vegetable used more for its stems than its leaves.

ginger

fresh called green or root ginger; thick gnarled root of a tropical plant.

ground also called powdered ginger; used as a flavouring in baking but cannot substitute for fresh ginger.

hazelnuts also known as filberts; plump, grape-sized, rich, sweet nut having a brown skin that is removed by rubbing heated nuts together vigorously in a tea-towel.

hoisin sauce a thick, sweet and spicy chinese barbecue sauce made from salted fermented soy beans, onions and garlic. Available from supermarkets and Asian food shops.

horseradish cream a commercially prepared creamy paste consisting of grated horseradish, vinegar, oil and sugar.

kaffir lime leaves also called bai magrood; looks like two glossy dark green leaves joined end to end to form a rounded hourglass shape. Sold fresh, dried or frozen; dried leaves are less potent so double the number if using them instead of fresh; a strip of fresh lime peel can replace each kaffir leaf.

kecap manis a dark, thick sweet soy sauce. Its sweetness is derived from the addition of molasses or palm sugar.

kumara the polynesian name of an orange-fleshed sweet potato often confused with yam.

lamb, backstrap also called eye of loin; the larger fillet from a row of loin chops or cutlets.

lemon grass a tall, clumping, lemon-tasting and smelling, sharp-edged tropical grass; the white lower part of the stem is used, finely chopped. Available in Asian food shops and supermarkets.

lentils dried pulses identified and named after their colour (red, brown, yellow).

macadamias fairly large, slightly soft, buttery rich nut. Store in the fridge to prevent their high oil content turning them rancid.

maple syrup distilled from the sap of maple trees. Maple-flavoured or pancake syrup is not an adequate substitute for the real thing.

mayonnaise we use whole-egg mayonnaise.

merguez sausages originating in Tunisia, this spicy sausage is made with beef or lamb and identified by its uncooked chilli-red colour.

mesclun a commercial assortment of young green leaves (rocket, mizuna, radicchio, baby spinach, oak leaf, curly endive and mignonette) and sometimes sold as spring salad mix.

mirin a Japanese champagne-coloured cooking wine, made of glutinous rice and alcohol. Used just for cooking and should not be confused with sake.

mizuna Japanese, frizzy salad leaves with a delicate mustard flavour.

mushrooms

button small, cultivated white mushrooms with a mild flavour.

oyster also known as abalone; grey-white mushrooms shaped like a fan. Prized for their smooth texture and subtle, oyster-like flavour.

shiitake *fresh*, are also called chinese black, forest or golden oak mushrooms. Although cultivated, they have the earthiness and taste of wild mushrooms. *dried* also called donko or dried chinese mushrooms. Uniquely meaty in flavour; rehydrate before use.

swiss brown also called roman or cremini. Light to dark brown in colour with full-bodied flavour.

mustard

american bright yellow; sweet mustard containing mustard seeds, sugar, salt, spices and garlic.

dijon also called french; pale brown, creamy, distinctively flavoured, mild french mustard.

seeds available in black (also called brown) and white (also called yellow seeds). Black seeds are more pungent than white.

wholegrain also called seeded. A French-style coarse-grain mustard made from crushed mustard seeds and dijon-style french mustard.

noodles

fried deep-fried crispy egg noodles packaged in 50g or 100g packets.

hokkien also called stir-fry noodles; fresh wheat noodles resembling thick, yellow-brown spaghetti. No need for pre-cooking.

rice stick also called sen lek, ho fun or kway teow; comes in different widths (thin, wide), but all should be soaked in hot water to soften.

rice vermicelli also called sen mee, mei fun or bee hoon. Used in spring rolls and cold salads. Before use, soak in hot water until softened, boil briefly then rinse with hot water.

soba thin, pale-brown Japanese noodle; made from buckwheat and wheat flour. Available dried, fresh and flavoured (such as green tea).

nori a dried seaweed used in Japanese cooking as a flavouring, garnish or for sushi. Sold in thin sheets, plain or toasted (yaki-nori).

oil

cooking spray we use a cholesterol-free spray made from canola oil.

olive made from ripened olives. *Extra virgin* and *virgin* are the first and second press, respectively and are considered the best; reference to "extra light" or "light" is to taste not fat levels.

peanut pressed from ground peanuts; most commonly used in Asian cooking because of its high smoke point.

sesame made from toasted, crushed, white sesame seeds.

vegetable any oil sourced from plants.

onions

fried onion/shallots found in cellophane bags or jars at Asian food shops.

green also called scallion or (incorrectly) shallot; an immature onion picked before the bulb has formed, having a long, bright-green edible stalk.

purple shallots also called asian shallots; related to the onion but resembes garlic. Thin-layered and intensely flavoured.

red also called spanish, red spanish or bermuda onion; a sweet-flavoured, large, purple-red onion.

spring crisp, narrow green-leafed tops and a round sweet white bulb larger than green onions.

oyster sauce thick, richly flavoured brown sauce made from oysters and their brine, cooked with salt and soy sauce, and thickened.

pancetta an Italian unsmoked bacon.

paprika ground dried sweet red capsicum.

pecans native to the USA; are golden brown, buttery and rich.

pepitas the pale green kernels of dried pumpkin seeds; can be bought plain or salted.

pine nuts also called pignoli; not a nut but the small, cream-coloured kernel from pine cones.

pistachios green, delicately flavoured nuts inside hard off-white shells. Available salted or unsalted in their shells, and shelled.

plum sauce a thick, sweet and sour dipping sauce made from plums, vinegar, sugar, chillies and spices.

pork

american-style spareribs well-trimmed mid-loin ribs.

belly fatty cut sold in rashers or in a piece, with or without rind or bone.

butterfly steaks skinless, boneless mid-loin chop, split in half and flattened.

potato

kipfler small, finger-shaped, nutty flavour.

new also called chats; not a separate variety but an early harvest with very thin skin.

prosciutto unsmoked Italian ham; salted, air-cured and aged, it is usually eaten uncooked.

radicchio Italian in origin; a member of the

chicory family. The dark burgundy leaves and strong, bitter flavour can be cooked or eaten raw in salads.

rice, basmati a white, fragrant long-grained rice; its grains fluff up when cooked. Wash several times before cooking.

risoni is a very small, rice-shaped pasta similar to orzo.

rocket also called arugula, rugula and rucola; peppery green salad leaf. Baby rocket leaves are smaller and less peppery.

sake made from fermented rice; if not available, use dry sherry, brandy or vermouth.

sambal oelek also ulek or olek; Indonesian in origin, this is a salty paste made from ground chillies and vinegar.

seafood

balmain bugs also known as slipper or shovelnose lobster, or southern bay lobster; crustacean, a type of crayfish. Substitute with moreton bay bugs, king prawns or scampi.

barramundi found in fresh and coastal waters in Australia's tropical north, weighing an average 4kg; also farmed commercially, are a firm, moist white fish best served whole. Substitute with nile perch.

blue-eye also known as deep sea trevalla or

trevally and blue-eye cod; thick, moist white-fleshed fish.

bream (yellowfin) also called silver or black bream, seabream or surf bream; soft, moist white flesh. Substitute with snapper or ocean perch.

sardines also called pilchards; small silvery fish with soft, oily flesh. Substitute with garfish.

squid or calamari; a type of mollusc. Buy squid hoods for quicker preparation and cooking.

swordfish also called broadbill. Substitute with yellowfin or bluefin tuna or mahi mahi.

white fish means non-oily fish. This category includes bream, whiting, flathead, snapper, ling, dhufish and redfish.

soy sauce made from fermented soybeans. Several variations (dark and light) are available in Asian food shops and supermarkets; we use Japanese soy sauce unless stated otherwise.

spinach also known as english spinach and incorrectly, silver beet. Baby spinach leaves are best eaten raw in salads; larger leaves should be added last and cooked until barely wilted.

star anise is a dried star-shaped pod; its seeds have an astringent aniseed flavour.

sugar

brown an extremely soft, fine granulated sugar; retains molasses for its characteristic colour and flavour.

palm also called nam tan pip, jaggery, jawa or gula melaka; made from the sap of the sugar palm tree. Light brown to black in colour and usually sold in rock-hard cakes; brown sugar can be used instead.

tamarind the tamarind tree produces clusters of hairy brown pods, each of which is filled with seeds and a viscous pulp, that are dried and pressed into the blocks of tamarind found in Asian food shops.

tofu

firm made by compressing bean curd to remove most of the water. Good used in stir-fries as it can be tossed without disintegrating. Can also be flavoured, preserved in rice wine or brine.

silken not a type of tofu but reference to the manufacturing process of straining soybean liquid through silk; this denotes best quality.

turmeric also known as kamin; is a rhizome related to galangal and ginger. Grate or pound to release its somewhat acrid aroma and pungent flavour. Known for the golden colour it imparts, fresh turmeric can be substituted with the more commonly found dried powder.

vietnamese mint

not a mint at all, but a pungent and peppery narrow-leafed member of the buckwheat family.

vinegar

apple cider made from fermented apples.

balsamic originally from Modena, Italy, there are now many on the market ranging in pungency and quality depending on how, and for how long, they have been aged. Quality is determined up to a point by price; use the most expensive sparingly.

malt made from fermented malt and beech shavings.

rice a colourless vinegar made from fermented rice and flavoured with sugar and salt. Also called seasoned rice vinegar; use sherry instead.

wasabi an asian horseradish used to make the pungent, green-coloured sauce; sold as powder or paste.

watercress member of the cress family, a large group of peppery greens; highly perishable, it must be used as soon as possible after purchase.

wombok also called chinese cabbage, peking or napa cabbage; elongated with pale green, crinkly leaves.

yogurt we use plain full-cream yogurt unless stated otherwise.

zucchini also known as courgette.

index

395

conversion chart

MEASURES

One Australian metric measuring cup holds approximately 250ml, one Australian metric tablespoon holds 20ml, one Australian metric teaspoon holds 5ml.

The difference between one country's measuring cups and another's is within a two- or three-teaspoon variance, and will not affect your cooking results.North America, New Zealand and the United Kingdom use a 15ml tablespoon.

All cup and spoon measurements are level. The most accurate way of measuring dry ingredients is to weigh them. When measuring liquids, use a clear glass or plastic jug with the metric markings.

We use large eggs with an average weight of 60g.

LIQUID MEASURES

METRIC	IMPERIAL
30ml	1 fluid oz
60ml	2 fluid oz
100ml	3 fluid oz
125ml	4 fluid oz
150ml	5 fluid oz (¼ pint/1 gill)
190ml	6 fluid oz
250ml	8 fluid oz
300ml	10 fluid oz (½ pint)
500ml	16 fluid oz
600ml	20 fluid oz (1 pint)
1000ml (1 litre)	1¾ pints

LENGTH MEASURES

METRIC	IMPERIAL
3mm	⅛in
6mm	¼in
1cm	½in
2cm	¾in
2.5cm	1in
5cm	2in
6cm	2½in
8cm	3in
10cm	4in
13cm	5in
15cm	6in
18cm	7in
20cm	8in
23cm	9in
25cm	10in
28cm	11in
30cm	12in (1ft)

DRY MEASURES

METRIC	IMPERIAL
15g	½oz
30g	1oz
60g	2oz
90g	3oz
125g	4oz (¼lb)
155g	5oz
185g	6oz
220g	7oz
250g	8oz (½lb)
280g	9oz
315g	10oz
345g	11oz
375g	12oz (¾lb)
410g	13oz
440g	14oz
470g	15oz
500g	16oz (1lb)
750g	24oz (1½lb)
1kg	32oz (2lb)

OVEN TEMPERATURES

These oven temperatures are only a guide for conventional ovens.
For fan-forced ovens, check the manufacturer's manual.

	°C (CELSIUS)	°F (FAHRENHEIT)	GAS MARK
Very slow	120	250	½
Slow	150	275 – 300	1 – 2
Moderately slow	160	325	3
Moderate	180	350 – 375	4 – 5
Moderately hot	200	400	6
Hot	220	425 – 450	7 – 8
Very hot	240	475	9

399

General manager Christine Whiston
Editorial director Susan Tomnay
Creative director Hieu Chi Nguyen
Editor Stephanie Kistner
Designer Caryl Wiggins
Food director Pamela Clark
Recipe consultant Louise Patniotis
Associate food editor Alex Somerville
Nutritional information Belinda Farlow
Director of sales Brian Cearnes
Marketing manager Bridget Cody
Business analyst Rebecca Varela
Operations manager David Scotto
Production manager Victoria Jefferys
International rights enquiries Laura Bamford
lbamford@acpuk.com

ACP Books are published by ACP Magazines
a division of PBL Media Pty Limited
Group publisher, Women's lifestyle Pat Ingram
Director of sales, Women's lifestyle Lynette Phillips
Commercial manager, Women's lifestyle Seymour Cohen
Marketing director, Women's lifestyle Matthew Dominello
Public relations manager, Women's lifestyle Hannah Deveraux
Creative director, Events, Women's lifestyle Luke Bonnano
Research Director, Women's lifestyle Justin Stone
ACP Magazines, Chief Executive officer Scott Lorson
PBL Media, Chief Executive officer Ian Law

Produced by ACP Books, Sydney.
Published by ACP Books, a division of ACP Magazines Ltd.
54 Park St, Sydney NSW Australia 2000. GPO Box 4088, Sydney, NSW 2001.
Phone +61 2 9282 8618 Fax +61 2 9267 9438
acpbooks@acpmagazines.com.au www.acpbooks.com.au
Printed by Toppan Printing Co., China.

Australia Distributed by Network Services, GPO Box 4088, Sydney, NSW 2001.
Phone +61 2 9282 8777 Fax +61 2 9264 3278 networkweb@networkservicescompany.com.au
United Kingdom Distributed by Australian Consolidated Press (UK),
10 Scirocco Close, Moulton Park Office Village, Northampton, NN3 6AP.
Phone +44 1604 642 200 Fax +44 1604 642 300
books@acpuk.com www.acpuk.com
New Zealand Distributed by Netlink Distribution Company, ACP Media Centre, Cnr Fanshawe
and Beaumont Streets, Westhaven, Auckland. PO Box 47906, Ponsonby, Auckland, NZ.
Phone +64 9 366 9966 Fax 0800 277 412 ask@ndc.co.nz
South Africa Distributed by PSD Promotions, 30 Diesel Road Isando, Gauteng Johannesburg.
PO Box 1175, Isando 1600, Gauteng Johannesburg.
Phone +27 11 392 6065/6/7 Fax +27 11 392 6079/80 orders@psdprom.co.za
Canada Distributed by Publishers Group Canada
Order Desk & Customer Service 9050 Shaughnessy Street, Vancouver BC V6P 6E5
Phone (800) 663 5714 Fax (800) 565 3770 service@raincoast.com

Title: Grill: the Australian women's weekly/food director, Pamela Clark; editor, Stephanie Kistner
Publisher: Sydney: ACP Books, 2008
ISBN: 978-1-86396-756-3 (pbk)
Notes: Includes index
Subjects: Barbecue cookery
Other authors/contributors: Clark, Pamela; Kistner, Stephanie
Also titled: Australian women's weekly
Dewey number: 641.5784
© ACP Magazines Ltd 2008
ABN 18 053 273 546

To order books, phone 136 116 (within Australia).
Send recipe enquiries to: askpamela@acpmagazines.com.au

Front cover Barbecued prawns with chilli lime dressing, page 231
Front cover photographer Rob Palmer
Front cover stylist Jane Hann
Front cover food preparation Ariarne Bradshaw
Illustrations Hannah Blackmore
Back cover photographer Joshua Dasey
Back cover stylist Margot Braddon